THE SAFE AND CARING CHURCH NURSERY

by Jennifer Root Wilger

Loveland, Colorado

DEDICATION

- *To my grandfather, Orrin Root, for inspiring me with his lifelong commitment to Christian education.*

- *To my husband, Tom Wilger, for encouraging me to write a book and supporting me while I did it.*

- *To my son, Micah Orrin Wilger, for teaching me how much and how quickly babies can learn.*

- *To Sarah and Susanna, for bringing home to me the eternal significance of sharing Jesus' love with children.*

The Safe and Caring Church Nursery

Copyright © 1998 Jennifer Root Wilger

Visit our Web site: **www.grouppublishing.com**

CREDITS
Book Acquisitions Editor: Paul Woods
Editor: Beth Rowland Wolf
Senior Editor: Christine Yount
Chief Creative Officer: Joani Schultz
Copy Editor: Debbie Gowensmith
Designer and Art Director: Jean Bruns
Cover Art Director: Jeff A. Storm
Cover Designer: Elise Lansdon
Computer Graphic Artist: Joyce Douglas
Cover Photographer: Craig DeMartino
Illustrator: Benrei Huang
Production Manager: Peggy Naylor

Library of Congress Cataloging-in-Publication Data
Wilger, Jennifer Root.
    The safe and caring church nursery / by Jennifer Root Wilger.
      p.   cm.
    Includes bibliographical references.
    ISBN 0-7644-2025-9 (alk. paper)
    1. Christian education of preschool children. I. Title.
BV1539.W55 1997   97-32378
268' .432--dc21   CIP

10 9 8 7 6   07 06 05 04

Printed in the United States of America.

Acknowledgments

*"Now you are the body of Christ, and
each one of you is a part of it"*
(1 CORINTHIANS 12:27).

The **Safe and Caring Church Nursery** was written with the help of dozens of parents and nursery workers in churches around the country. As you read the book, I know you'll join me in thanking God for their commitment and dedication to the little ones in their care. I'd also like to extend special thanks to the following churches, organizations, and individuals for going out of their way to share their nursery plans, programs, and experiences with me and with all of you.

Barbara Curtis
Novato, California

Teresa Strawn
Loveland, Colorado

Boulder Valley
Christian Church
Boulder, Colorado

Dawn Martin
*Scottsdale Bible Church
Scottsdale, Arizona*

Bonnie Temple
*Eugene Christian
Fellowship
Eugene, Oregon*

Tammy Ross
*First Baptist Church
Columbia, Tennessee*

Barbara Long
*First Baptist Church
Decatur, Georgia*

Reverend Scott Helferty
& Nina Catelli Vincent
*Grace Episcopal Church
New Bedford,
Massachusetts*

Joan Gray
*Columbia Presbyterian
Church
Decatur, Georgia*

Connie Sylvester
*Christ Community
Church
Charlottesville, Virginia*

Linda Byram
*Overlake Christian
Church
Kirkland, Washington*

Erin Healy
*Christian Parenting
Today*

Christine Yount
*Children's Ministry
Magazine*

Every church nursery ministry is different. The author, publisher, and the individuals listed here have taken care to acquaint you and your church with the safety issues you'll encounter as you build your nursery ministry, but we know we can't possibly anticipate the individual needs and circumstances of every church. Therefore, we kindly remind you that each church is responsible for its use and implementation of the material presented in *The Safe and Caring Church Nursery,* including all liability that may result from any accidents.

Contents

Introduction

"If parents are not comfortable with the care their children are receiving, they will not concentrate on the services or fully worship God. They might not even come back to the church."

PAM COOPER
MOULTRIE, GEORGIA

As a parent, I am a frequent user of my church's nursery. My husband and I look forward to participating in worship together, and we rely on our church's nursery workers to care for our son while we do so. Although Micah, eighteen months old as I write, doesn't fully comprehend what Mommy and Daddy do in church, he knows what church means. "Class...church...teach...love...Jesus...slide," he tells me as we get ready for church each Sunday morning.

Slide? At this stage, Micah's favorite thing about our church nursery is the toddler-sized plastic slide. And as silly as it may seem, we thank God for that slide because it makes the transition to the nursery just a little easier. The slide (and the playhouse and the tricycle and the blocks and the other toys) makes the nursery a fun place for Micah to play. But the toys and equipment in the nursery aren't just for playing. These things help Micah learn that church is a happy place where he can discover new things about God and the world God created...*if a loving teacher helps him make the connection.*

In this book, you'll find scores of practical ideas to help you ensure that your church nursery is making the connection. Urban or rural, large or small—across denominational lines the concerns are the same. From Tim in North Carolina: "Your church nursery is a magnet to attract young families to your church." From Joan in Georgia: "We know the nursery is the most important room in the church." From Barbara in California: "The nursery may be the first bit of Jesus that people see." For families with small children, the quality of your church nursery is critical. Whether you're starting a nursery from scratch or building on an existing program, *The Safe and Caring Church Nursery* can help you turn your nursery into a thriving, dynamic ministry.

Science and society are just now beginning to realize what parents, child-care workers, and pastors have always known: Tiny children can learn! The media is abuzz with the news that children learn more during their first three years of life than in any other time span. Armed with the latest research, parents are talking, reading, and singing to their children at every opportunity.

The safe and caring church nursery will provide well-prepared facilities and well-trained, loving workers to stand alongside and support parents as they seek to nurture their children. For their children are *our* children, and—perhaps more importantly—they're also God's children. God has made each child special, unique, and teachable. I pray that this book will guide you as you minister to the precious little ones God has placed in your care.

Section 1:

PREPARING A PLACE

Finding and preparing a room for your nursery

DO BABIES TRAVEL FIRST CLASS?

Selecting a room for your nursery

"If the nursery is to be an evangelistic outreach, it's important to spare no expense."

BARBARA CURTIS
NOVATO, CALIFORNIA

O n a recent visit to my grandmother, I attended a church in central California. Since Grandma is in a wheelchair, I was on my own to search for the church nursery. The church was small, so I was confident I could find my way. Finding no signs or other information to guide me, I headed away from the sanctuary and into what I assumed was the Sunday school classroom area. After wandering down a hall and opening a few doors, I found the three-year-olds and the kitchen, but no nursery.

Knowing that eighteen-month-old Micah would be much happier sitting on a rocking horse than in a pew, I continued down the dimly lit hall and around a corner. A few unlabeled doors later, I noticed a door with an index card taped to it. Written on the card, in what looked like an older child's handwriting, were the words "Babies are in here."

I turned the doorknob slowly, fearful of what I might find behind the door in that dark hall. Was there a reason the nursery seemed hidden? Was I about to enter every parent's nightmare? And how would I explain to Grandma if I decided the nursery was unsuitable for my son?

Fortunately, the nursery was fine. It wasn't fancy or spacious, but it was clean and equipped with appropriate toys—including the familiar plastic slide. Micah would be safe and even happy there while I joined Grandma for worship.

I only get to visit Grandma once or twice a year, so the location of her church's nursery doesn't greatly affect me. Besides, now I know where to find it. But what about more frequent visitors? What about the new family in the community looking for a church home? Or the single mom who has never before set foot in a church? If she doesn't find the nursery, she might not make it to the sanctuary.

From Hide-and-Seek to Seek-and-Find

Location is an important factor to consider when selecting a room for your church's nursery. Ideally, every church nursery would be directly adjacent to the main worship area, clearly marked by a "BABIES ARE IMPORTANT IN OUR CHURCH!" sign. Reverend Scott Helferty of Grace Episcopal Church in New Bedford, Massachusetts, formerly served in a church with the next-best thing. "The nursery was directly above the entrance to the sanctuary. And it had a sound-proof glass wall so the children could see into the service," Scott explained.

The nursery at Grace Episcopal, where Scott currently serves, is more typical—an ample, well-equipped classroom space in Grace's church-school area that is sectioned off from the next room by a fold-ing divider. But Scott is still vexed by the visibility problem. "Unfortunately, at our church traffic flows in and out of the building without passing by the nursery or other learning areas. Parishioners know where to find the nursery, but visitors don't necessarily know about it." Not only do visitors have trouble finding the nursery, but they may not even know that classes or care is available for babies if they've never been to the church before.

For all the time, devotion, prayer, and yes, even money you put into your church's nursery program, you certainly want people to be able to find it! So if you're just starting a nursery program or are consid-ering moving your nursery rooms, choose an easy-to-find location. Try putting your nursery...

- near the main worship area;
- near an outside door (handy for nature walks, important for fire safety, but locked from the outside to keep strangers from entering);
- near the restrooms;
- near the adult Sunday school rooms; or
- near the entrance to your children's Christian education or Sunday school area.

If you're working with an existing facility (as most churches are), put your best foot forward by directing parents to your nursery in one or more of the following ways:

Label the doors. Put signs on nursery doors. If the door is usually partially or completely opened, put a sign nearby on a wall. Make the signs as readable, attractive, and permanent as your budget allows. This sign will be your first contact with parents and an affirmation that they've found what they're looking for. Remember "Babies are in here"? It was cheap, it was easy, but it did absolutely nothing to reassure me that I had found a place where I could comfortably leave my child.

Nursery-door signs should be readable from a distance and should identify the age group that is cared for in that room. For an added touch, include clip art or pictures of babies. If parents are within reading distance, they'll have no question about whether they've found their destination. But to get them to this point, begin directing them to the nursery when they first enter the church building.

Post additional signs. Especially if the nursery or Christian education area isn't easily visible from your church's entrance, post additional signs. Place the signs at eye level in any hallways or stairways that parents might pass through on their way to the nursery. These signs, too, should be easy to read and should include directional arrows as needed. But in addition to directing parents to the nursery's location, you can also use the signs to build excitement about the nursery. The following ideas will help your signs welcome and direct parents through your building.

Photos—Create a sign that says, "Come downstairs and join us," and include a photo (five-by-seven or larger) of a baby in your church—or the whole nursery class. Close-ups of caring workers might also help put concerned parents at ease.

Borders—Create a fun border for your sign with pictures of babies or baby items such as rattles, pacifiers, or teddy bears.

Scripture verses—If your nursery or children's department has a theme verse, include it on the signs. Also include simple mission statements or teaching goals.

Provide lobby information. Many churches set up tables with information about ministries and activities in the main entry area. If your church does this, include nursery information. In addition to door and directional signs, Boulder Valley Christian Church in Boulder, Colorado, posts a listing of all Sunday school classes with room numbers. Knowing the nursery's room number gives parents reassurance that they're heading the right direction. If you want to go the extra mile, provide a building map labeled with room numbers and class names.

Use ushers or greeters. Signs will do the job, but if you really want to welcome new families, designate special greeters for families with babies. Set apart these "nursery guides" with name tags or even brightly colored nursery-guide badges.

It only takes a few seconds for greeters to say, "Welcome to our church. We're glad you're here. May I direct you to our nursery?" Greeters can then provide spoken directions—or, better yet, can lead the parents to the nursery. As they lead new families through your church, they can also point out other areas of interest such as

● classrooms for older children;

● adult classrooms;

● locations of parenting classes, moms' groups, or other relevant ministries;

● the church office;

● the fellowship hall (especially if your church provides coffee or refreshments after services);

● the main worship area; and

● restrooms.

A nursery guide can be anyone in your church with a friendly smile and a love for children. Teenagers make great nursery guides! When I was ten years old, my family moved from California to Oregon. I can still remember the name and face of the high school student who met us at the door of the church that would become our new church home. Patiently and happily, he guided us first to the nursery and then to the appropriate Sunday school classes for all five older children. To this day, my mother insists that Kenny Jones is the reason we chose that church.

Remember, you may never get a second chance to make a good first impression. So choose your nursery location carefully, and then provide plenty of friendly directions to help folks find their way.

Can Less Be More?

You want parents to be pleased with your nursery facilities. It's important that they feel comfortable leaving their babies in the nursery. But your nursery's primary mission is to provide excellent,

Christ-centered care for the babies, not to showcase the latest in nursery paraphernalia. In other words, if your nursery is still sporting last year's wallpaper patterns (or no wallpaper at all), the babies won't care.

I recently had the pleasure of meeting Barbara Curtis, author of Christian parenting materials and mother of eleven. Barbara has had a lot of babies in a lot of nurseries! But as we talked, she never described a single nursery's appearance. Instead, she stressed the importance of making the church nursery a financial priority within the church's overall budget. And she's right. But "financial priority" and "fancy nursery" don't necessarily go hand in hand. If you skimp on your nursery, parents will notice. But if your nursery expenditures bankrupt your church, you've accomplished nothing. An extravagant nursery in a small church will draw just as much negative criticism as an undersupplied nursery in a larger one.

You want your nursery to look cute and fun, warm and inviting. But above all, your church should provide clean, well-ventilated, well-lit rooms with plenty of space for young explorers to move around.

Cozy Corners to Exploratoriums

So how big does your nursery need to be? That depends on the number and ages of children who typically participate in your church's nursery program. The storage closet is definitely too small, and the fellowship hall is too large. Early-childhood experts recommend a minimum of thirty-five square feet of space per child. If your current room is much smaller than this, you may want to consider moving or adding additional rooms.

Subdividing your nursery by age or motor-skill development can sometimes ease crowded conditions. At Overlake Christian Church in Kirkland, Washington, nurseries for children under age two are available for infants, creepers (actively mobile babies), toddlers (beginning walkers), and run-abouts (confident walkers). Parents usually decide where to place their children. Unless you have fewer than five children in your nursery program, it's generally best to provide at least one room for babies and one room for toddlers. The "Many Rooms" chart on pages 16 and 17 can help you find the right balance for your church.

Cleanliness Before Baby Mess

You've carefully considered the location and size of each room, and you've calculated the precise number of children per room. Now are you ready to open your nursery for business? Not quite. Before you move any furniture or equipment into the rooms (and at regular intervals afterward), give each room a thorough cleaning.

Inspect the paint. If the walls look dirty, clean and disinfect them. If paint is peeling, repaint the room. Don't forget to check the ceiling!

Sweep or vacuum all floors. Shampoo any carpeted areas.

Clean and disinfect any cabinets (inside and out), cubbyholes, or counter tops. Make sure cabinet knobs or handles are tightly attached.

Wash any windows, inside and out. Check to make sure locks work and all hardware is firmly attached. Inspect and replace screens if necessary.

Deodorize if necessary. If possible, use an unscented or mild deodorizer.

Once the room is clean, you'll also want to consider lighting, ventilation, and temperature control.

Lighting—Natural lighting is best. If your nursery has overly bright lighting, install a dimmer switch to soften the glare. For sleeping areas, turn off overhead lights and provide dim lamps or night lights. Plug them in where crawling babies can't reach them.

Ventilation—If your church has a central heating or air conditioning system, fresh air will probably circulate through the room regularly. If not, bring in small fans. Remember to place the fans and their cords well out of babies' reach!

Temperature control—Keep the room temperature between sixty-eight and seventy-eight degrees Fahrenheit. Ideally, the nursery should have its own thermostat. If your temperature control is in another area, talk with others who use that part of the building to agree on a thermostat setting.

Although selecting and preparing a room for a nursery may be a big job, it's only the beginning of creating a safe and caring nursery. Once your room is clean and comfortable, you're ready to make it baby-friendly. Now the fun begins!

MANY ROOMS

In my Father's house, there are many rooms...how many of them should be full of babies?

Total number of children	Number of children under 12 months	Number of children 12-24 months	Recommended number of rooms	Recommended age/developmental subdivisions
5	up to 5	up to 5	1	Birth to 24 months
10	up to 10	up to 10	2	Infants (not yet walking) Toddlers (walking)
15	5-10	5-10	2	Infants (not yet walking) Toddlers (walking)
	10-15	up to 5	2-3	Infants (0-6 months) Crawlers (6-12 months) Toddlers (12-24 months)
20	up to 5	15-20	2-3	Infants (0-12 months) Walkers (12-18 months) Talkers (18-24 months)
	5-10	10-15	2-3	Infants (0-6 months) Crawlers (6-12 months) Toddlers (12-24 months)

20	10-15	5-10	3-4	Infants *(0-4 months)* Creepers *(4-8 months)* Crawlers *(8 months to walking)* Toddlers *(walking to 24 months)*
25	up to 5	20-25	3	Infants *(0-12 months)* Walkers *(12-18 months)* Talkers *(18-24 months)*
	5-10	15-20	3-4	Infants *(0-6 months)* Crawlers *(6-12 months)* Walkers *(12-18 months)* Talkers *(18-24 months)*
	10-20	5-15	3-4	Infants *(0-4 months)* Creepers *(4-8 months)* Crawlers *(8 months to walking)* Toddlers *(walking to 24 months)*
over 25	Few churches have space for more than 4 nursery rooms (most are lucky to secure and equip 2). If your church has more than 25 children under 2, you can increase your available space by offering nursery care at multiple services. Don't forget to recruit additional workers! You'll need at least 1 worker for every 3 infants, and at least 1 worker for every 4 toddlers.			

CRUISERS, NOT BRUISERS

Organizing and babyproofing your nursery for safety

"If the nursery is not up to standards, it says things about our church we don't want to say."

JOAN GRAY
DECATUR, GEORGIA

CPSC. NPSI. JPMA. Hmm...aren't nursery children a little young for word scrambles? Absolutely. But to concerned parents, these jumbled letters may mean something—they're abbreviations for three organizations that monitor the safety of children's products. The U.S. Consumer Product Safety Commission (CPSC), the National Playground Safety Institute (NPSI), and the Juvenile Products Manufacturers Association (JPMA) are just a few of the growing number of organizations dedicated to baby and child safety.

"If an accident is waiting to happen, your 2-year-old will find it," wrote Ellen Alcorn in Parents magazine. The same is true for toddlers, cruisers, crawlers, and generally any baby that lives and breathes! Although the task may seem daunting at first, you *must* babyproof your nursery facilities. You should check every wall, floor, window, door, cabinet, and counter top. Don't let the following excuses (or others) stop you from doing what's necessary to make your nursery as safe as possible.

But we've never had an accident. Hallelujah. And pray that you never do. But an accident-free history doesn't guarantee an accident-free future—especially if conditions in your nursery are unsafe. Your nursery's accident record is not unlike your driving record. The fact that you've never been in an auto accident doesn't keep you from maintaining auto insurance. Babyproofing is an important part of your nursery's "insurance" to prevent accidents from happening.

But the guidelines change so frequently. If you're tempted to think that no one can possibly keep up with all the current safety guidelines, think again. Bookstores and newsstands are flooded with parenting books and magazines that tell parents how to babyproof their homes. Parents know what to look for in a safe baby environment—and if they don't find it in your church nursery, they'll be out the door before you can say "peekaboo." If you're unsure whether your nursery facilities and equipment meet current safety guidelines, call the U.S. Consumer Product Safety Commission at 1-800-638-2772 or visit the organization's Web site at http://www.cpsc.gov. Much of the safety information you'll find in this book has been obtained from these CPSC sources.

But we can't afford to keep replacing our equipment. You may not have to. Safety gadgets may abound, but by themselves they're no substitute for proper supervision. You may be able to solve your safety problems by adding additional workers, rearranging furniture and equipment, or simply removing unsafe items from your nursery.

But we don't have space to put everything away, and the babies won't notice the clutter... Maybe not and maybe so. The sleeping newborns may not notice, but older infants and toddlers will notice, approach, and attack it. And their parents will most certainly notice.

Our family recently attended a church dinner. Since the event was outside the scheduled service times, the nursery was closed. But child care was provided in one of the preschool rooms. When I took Micah to the room, I encountered counter tops cluttered with papers, toy baskets overflowing with toys, and two TV/VCR carts in the middle of the room. Envisioning all sorts of nightmares—broken video equipment, shredded Sunday school curriculum, toddlers pinned by the heavy cart—I chose to stay in the room so at least my child would be safe and out of trouble.

Unwanted clutter hinders safety—and learning—for older children and adults as well as babies. The only equipment in your nursery should be nursery equipment. Remember—cruisers, not bruisers!

Convinced? Then you're ready for *The Safe and Caring Church Nursery's* all-excuses-aside, check-your-pride-with-the-diaper-bags "Floor-to-Ceiling Nursery Safety Checklist" (pp. 20-21). (The items on this list deal mostly with the physical features of your nursery room. Section 2 contains safety checklists for specific nursery equipment.) If babyproofing seems like a big job, it is. Just ask any parent! But once you've done it, you'll be able to rest assured that your church's little ones will be safe and comfortable while in your care.

FLOOR-TO-CEILING NURSERY SAFETY CHECKLIST

Floors

_____ I have crawled around the room to survey it from a baby's perspective.

_____ I have removed any small objects that babies can pick up and put into their mouths.

_____ I have inspected the rugs to see that they have nonskid, nonstick backing. If they don't, I have removed or replaced them.

_____ I have cleaned all carpets, rugs, and floors.

Walls

_____ I have confirmed that the walls are painted with lead-free paint.

_____ I have inspected the walls for peeling or chipped paint and have repainted or covered problem spots. (Large bulletin boards work great for this.)

_____ I have inspected the walls for loose or peeling wallpaper and reattached or covered problem spots.

_____ I have cleaned all the walls.

First Aid

_____ I have placed a stocked first-aid kit out of children's reach.

_____ I have provided phone numbers for local poison control and hospital emergency rooms. And I have posted the location of the nearest telephone.

Fire Safety

_____ I have installed and tested a smoke detector and a carbon monoxide detector.

_____ I have placed a fire extinguisher out of children's reach.

_____ I have provided a map to the nearest outside exit.

_____ I have routed electrical cords safely out of walking areas. (Walking on electrical cords—even if they're covered with rugs or carpeting—can break their wiring and cause fires.)

Furniture and Fixtures

_____ I have shielded old-style radiators to protect children from being burned.

_____ I have stored plastic bags, diaper-changing supplies, and cleaning supplies in latched cabinets or out of children's reach.

_____ I have covered all electrical outlets with safety plugs.

_____ I have removed all electrical cords from children's reach.

_____ I have anchored or secured all furniture and shelves to prevent children from pulling them over.

_____ I have placed padding on any sharp corners or edges.

_____ I have removed all poisonous plants and placed any non-poisonous live plants out of children's reach.

_____ I have removed thumbtacks and staples from bulletin boards within children's reach.

_____ I have checked all cabinet and furniture knobs to see that they're securely fastened.

_____ I have removed any unnecessary furnishings or supplies from the room.

Windows

_____ I have inspected windows and screens to ensure that they're securely fastened.

_____ I have moved furniture and equipment away from window areas.

_____ I have secured drapery or window-covering cords out of children's reach.

Doors

_____ I have installed locks or latches on any doors that children can reach and possibly open.

_____ I have removed or replaced doorstops with removable caps.

Ceiling

_____ I have inspected ceiling tiles to ensure they're firmly in place.

_____ I have removed, inspected, cleaned, and replaced all overhead lighting fixtures.

_____ I have inspected textured ceilings and removed any loose plaster.

After you've completed this checklist, file it for future reference—you may need it again. Or post it in or near your church nursery to let parents know that their children's safety is your first concern.

Safety Extra:
THE SAFE AND HAPPY PLAYGROUND

If your nursery department includes toddlers and preschoolers, you may choose to provide outdoor play areas for sunny-day play. Outdoor play areas can range from grassy lawns with portable plastic toys to full playgrounds with permanent play structures. The National Playground Safety Institute (NPSI) estimates that more than 170,000 serious injuries and approximately twenty deaths occur on playgrounds each year.

A properly maintained playground can be a lot of fun for young children, but an unsafe play place will inevitably lead to disaster. If your playground is a safety hazard, no one should play on it—especially not nursery-aged children. In most cases, nursery-aged children will be safer (and probably just as happy) spending most of their time playing on age-appropriate, smaller-scale, indoor equipment, supplemented by an occasional outdoor walk.

For more information about outdoor playground safety, contact

National Recreation and Park Association
22377 Belmont Ridge Road
Ashburn, VA 20148-4501
(703) 820-4940

BEYOND BUNNIES AND BEARS

··

Bright, lively ideas
for nursery décor

*"Nursery décor is becoming more and more
important. Parents are used to day cares—
and even McDonald's [restaurants]—that are
bright and beautifully decorated."*
LINDA BYRAM
KIRKLAND, WASHINGTON

Soft, fluffy cottontail bunnies. Smiling bears clutching bunches of brightly colored balloons. With one glance at these designs, anyone who peeks in the door can conclude, "I've found the baby room." The look of your nursery communicates a lot. A dull, drab nursery can look cold and uncaring—even if it's staffed by loving workers. A brightly decorated, home-like room lights up parents' faces and warms their hearts.

But what about babies, the real occupants of the room? Does nursery décor even make a difference to them? Yes! Visual stimulation is an important part of infant growth and development. Babies are born with immature vision and gradually learn to distinguish objects, patterns, and colors. A well-thought-out, nicely decorated nursery may actually make a small (but positive) contribution to the babies' developing vision.

What kind of decorating scheme will best accomplish this purpose? For infant rooms, think simple and think contrast. Despite the preponderance of pastel baby products available, babies respond best to bright colors or even simple black-and-white images. In *Your Child's Development From Birth Through Adolescence*, Richard Lansdown and Marjorie Walker point out that newborn babies have limited perception of color and at birth can only distinguish yellow, red, green, and turquoise from gray. By three months, babies appear to have full color perception. Although young babies may seem to study faces and other images, they won't be able to identify small details in pictures until around eighteen months, so keep patterns and pictures large and bold.

Every church wants a cozy, home-like nursery environment, but few churches believe they can afford to create it. Overlake Christian Church in Kirkland, Washington, has thousands of members and hundreds of volunteer nursery workers. But nursery director Linda Byram is still concerned about the cost of decorating the nursery in the church's new building, currently under construction. She hopes to get parents on board to help finance and carry out her decorating plan— a simple Noah's ark mural. "Of all the things I looked into, a mural seemed the most reasonable," she explained.

Linda Byram is not alone. Of all the decorating ideas I've seen or heard, murals popped up most often. They're inexpensive, relatively easy to do, and, once finished, they give the room a long-lasting, maintenance-free décor. Murals are one way to go. And below you'll find proven ideas to make your murals even better. You'll also find nine more creative decorating ideas. Low budget? No problem—most of the ideas included here can be done for one hundred dollars or less. So take this book to your nursery, look around, and start dreaming.

Ten Ways to Brighten Your Nursery

1. Paint a mural. Mary Davis, a twenty-five-year children's ministry veteran from Iowa, painted a mural of Jesus and the children on one toddler-room wall. One- and two-year-olds would go over and touch Jesus or give him "hugs" by putting their faces against him. For story time, Mary put a blanket near the mural so the children could "sit with Jesus."

Bonnie Temple, early childhood director at Eugene Christian Fellowship in Eugene, Oregon, is also a big fan of interactive murals for toddlers. She suggests including doors for children to knock on, hidden pictures for children to find, or tables where children can pull up real chairs. She also points out that you never know where you might find artistic talent; the murals at Eugene Christian Fellowship were painted by the church janitor.

Wondering where to start? Linda Byram suggests using an overhead projector to create a mural image. Photocopy an image onto an overhead transparency. Project the image onto the wall, and outline it with pencil. Then turn off the projector and paint the details. Looking for ideas? Try visiting a toy store, school-supply house, party store, or baby-furniture store for general baby-friendly themes. If you want a biblical theme, try Noah's ark or Jesus and the children.

2. Put up a wallpaper border. Wallpaper creates a finished look. But putting up wallpaper can be time-consuming, messy, and expensive. You can create a similar look with a fraction of the time, mess, and expense by opting for a wallpaper border. Hang borders along the top of the wall, mid-wall, or (if you can't afford to do the whole room) around door and window openings.

Choose a border with a simple, bright pattern. Although borders cost less than wallpaper, bordering a whole room can add up. Shop around. Check children's furniture stores, fabric and hobby stores, home-improvement stores, and discount stores such as Target and Wal-Mart.

3. Decorate with stencils. Most craft, hobby, and art-supply stores carry a good supply of stencils, paints, and brushes. Brightly colored stencils applied in a pattern can create a look similar to a wallpaper border. We chose to do stencils in Micah's room. The brightly colored animal parade we created is perfect for his toddler tastes, but someday he might want the animals to change to cars. If you think your nursery might move at some point, stencils are a good way to go. They're also easy for a nonartistic person (like me!) to do.

4. Use bulletin boards and wall hangings. Creating and maintaining bulletin board scenes can seem like a never-ending task. If you use bulletin boards, plan ahead for no more than four simple scenes a year. Although you may get tired of looking at them, the babies won't. For an even easier approach, Mary Davis suggests covering bulletin boards with brightly colored gingham or religious-print fabrics. "There's lots of Noah's ark material available," Mary points out, "even at Wal-Mart." Solid fabrics can be backgrounds to bright felt flowers, suns, or stars. Large, bright prints can stand alone.

Soft fabric sculptures or colorful quilts can also brighten up

NURSERY NOTE

Rub-on or stick-on decals are also available. These are extremely easy to use, but many of them picture cartoon, Disney, or super-hero characters. While these characters are cute and may be appropriate for home nurseries, it's a good idea to avoid them at church. Young children may have trouble distinguishing between fictional cartoon characters and real people from the Bible. So stick to generic animals or people for your stencils or decals.

walls—and require much less maintenance than bulletin boards. Except for the occasional washing, most wall hangings are maintenance free. Mary has even used uninflated Mylar balloons as wall or ceiling hangings. She says infants seem to enjoy the shiny reflections as much as the pictures printed on the balloons. Brightly colored baby play mats can also do double duty as decorations when not in use. Hang wall hangings near cribs or changing tables where babies will enjoy looking at them, but hang them high enough that children can't reach them.

5. Create animal or people paper chains. If you're low on money but high on people power, this idea's for you! With a little time and effort, you can create your own borders using animal or people chain patterns. If you want to make a border for your entire room, you'll need lots of chains (hence the high people-power quotient). To put up your border, mark a straight baseline along the wall, and then attach the chains with wallpaper paste.

For instructions and patterns, check out *Wild Animal Paper Chains* by Stewart and Sally Walton (Tupelo Books, 1993).

6. Decorate with baby prints. Hand or foot prints, that is. If the thought of stamping a six-month-old's hand all around your room sounds impossible, it probably is. Even a one-year-old is probably only good for about a dozen prints before breaking free and painting furniture, toys, and other children. (At age one, Micah barely held still long enough to cover a tote bag.) But two- or three-year-olds will probably enjoy making prints. And what a great way to teach service at an early age!

To create a two-year-old hand-print border in your nursery, arrange for a time that the two-year-olds and babies can switch rooms (you may have to move a few pieces of furniture). Cover the floors in your nursery, cover the two-year-olds with paint shirts, and print away. To keep children safe, have them make a border just above the baseboards or under windows. Adults won't strain their arms holding children up, children won't fall off ladders, and, best of all, babies will notice the bright prints as they crawl around the floor. Take time to explain what you're doing, and praise children for helping to make the nursery a fun place for babies to learn about God.

If the two-year-old project is more than you want to tackle, consider printing a few baby hand or foot prints and having a rubber stamp made. You may even be able to purchase a ready-made baby foot-print stamp. Use paint or ink to stamp a foot-print border on your walls.

7. Fill your room with all God's creatures. Put up four shelves where adults can easily reach them. About eighteen inches above each shelf, stencil or paint one of the following lines from *All Things Bright and Beautiful,* the poem by Cecil Frances Alexander.

> All things bright and beautiful,
> All creatures great and small,
> All things wise and wonderful,
> The Lord God made them all.

Collect a variety of stuffed animals, and store them on the shelves. Besides being decorative, the shelves provide storage for stuffed toys and remind nursery workers of God's wonderful creation. Be sure to dust the shelves—and the animals—regularly.

8. Show babies who God loves. Babies love faces—especially their own. Bonnie Temple suggests placing safety mirrors low, where babies can crawl or scoot over and see themselves. For older toddlers or two-year-olds, place mirrors near a box of dress-up clothes so children can see themselves all dressed up. Near each mirror, place a sign that says, "I see someone Jesus loves." Children won't be able to read them, but the words will remind workers to talk to children about Jesus as they play near the mirrors. The signs also let parents know that your nursery workers take time to share God's love with the children.

9. Paint your furniture. For toddler rooms, use nontoxic paint to paint child-sized tables and chairs in bright primary colors. And while you're at it, paint your baseboards. Even old furniture can look cheerful if it's painted.

10. Surround your babies with babies. Take close-up photographs of several babies, and have the photographs enlarged and dry-mounted. (If photographic enlargements are too expensive, get enlarged color photocopies.) Or frame an enlarged panoramic shot of all the babies lined up on a couch. Besides entertaining the babies, the photos will inspire parents and other volunteers.

For a three-dimensional approach, take action photos of babies scooting, crawling, and toddling. Get enlarged color photocopies, and mount them on cardboard or foam core. Then cut out the babies' pictures to create photo sculptures. Hang the sculptures on your wall or bulletin board—or in the hall that leads to your nursery.

Your room is clean. Your room is safe. And now your room is painted, papered, printed, pictured, or otherwise prepared. You're ready to bring in the baby gear!

Section 2:

FROM BARE ROOM TO BABY ZONE

Equipping and maintaining your nursery

BEHIND BARS

Cribs, playpens, and other essential equipment

"I have been to three different churches in our area. One had fairly well-staffed nurseries (infant/toddler, 2/4, 5/6), but the rooms themselves were something else. The cribs were outdated and unsafe, the floors were uncarpeted concrete, the toys were all at least 20 years old (complete with small parts and sharp edges) and they used walkers (!) and old ones at that."

"NANELCAM"
FROM AMERICA ONLINE

We began attending our current church as a young married couple and are now actively involved in several church ministries. Shortly after we added Micah to our family, we added him to the cradle roll. Because we already knew, loved, and trusted our church family, I confess I didn't scrutinize every last detail of the nursery. Since I embarked on writing this book, I've taken a closer look, and there are definitely a few things about our church nursery that I'd like to change. We're not about to leave the church over them, but parents without our history and commitment might.

Safety is a big, big deal to parents. Your church nursery—and the equipment in it—sends a loud message about how your church views young children and their families. Many families who visit your church have their children in day care, and they set their child-care expectations accordingly. Most day-care centers do an excellent job tending to children's physical, social, and even intellectual needs. The church nursery has the potential to do even more. That's because your church can also minister to children's spiritual needs—but only if parents perceive your nursery as a safe, comfortable place to leave their children. As Barbara Long—minister of childhood education at First Baptist Church in Decatur, Georgia, and a twenty-five-year veteran of children's ministry—put it, "If it's good enough for day care, it should be better for the church."

So what kind of equipment will send the right message? What will make parents think to themselves, "Wow! This is *better* than day care"? "Nanelcam" from America Online also said, "The second church [we visited] had poorly staffed (2 adults per 12+ children) but wonderful rooms...with newish toys and safe-looking cribs." We've already covered age groupings, and in Section 3 we'll get to staffing. Let's talk now about those safe-looking cribs (and other equipment).

What Parents Wish Their Churches Knew About Cribs...

"Safe-looking" is a highly subjective criterion. Parents aren't likely to question the safety of shiny new cribs adorned with the latest children's print fabrics. But they tend to hesitate at the sight of older cribs. Don't they realize you're on a budget?

Of course. Parents who bring their babies to the nursery know exactly what cribs cost. After all, they recently bought one themselves. And as they searched for the perfect crib to complete their baby's nursery, they were cautioned repeatedly, "Don't put your baby in an older, used crib." Churches should follow the same advice.

Why? Since 1973, the Consumer Product Safety Commission (CPSC) has revised its crib safety standards several times. In addition to the original requirements that addressed side height, slat spacing, and mattress fit, standards prohibiting hazardous cutouts in crib end panels were added in 1982. In 1986 and 1989, CPSC added voluntary standards to address additional hazards such as getting clothing entangled on corner posts on all cribs and structural and mechanical failure on full-size cribs. Standards to address structural and mechanical problems on non-full-size cribs are still in development.

According to CPSC, these standards have reduced infant deaths related to crib injuries from two hundred per year to about fifty per year. Most of the current deaths and injuries related to cribs occur in older, used cribs.

What Churches Can Do to Ease Parents' Concerns

The cribs in your nursery needn't be fancy or expensive, but they must be safe. How do you know if your cribs are safe? Ask around to find out how long the cribs have been in your nursery. If they haven't been replaced for twenty-five years or more (pre-1973), they're likely worn out as well as potentially unsafe. Cribs that date back to the late 1970s or early 1980s should definitely be checked for safety using the checklist on page 39. Cribs that are less than ten years old are probably safe, but they should also be checked. If you find you need to replace cribs, buy or acquire cribs that were manufactured after 1989. Check to see that a CPSC safety-approval label is in place.

Replace or remove any crib that's unsafe. Just do it—even if the crib looks perfectly all right to you. And if you can't afford to buy new cribs, try one of the following alternatives:

Purchase newer used cribs. Check garage sales and used-furniture stores for clean, well-kept, used cribs that meet current CPSC standards. Be sure to ask when the crib was originally purchased. If you can't find out the original purchase date, don't buy the crib.

Borrow cribs. Parents of babies soon become parents of preschoolers. Post a notice in your church's newsletter or preschool department requesting newer cribs. Many parents would be thrilled to have someone transport their cribs from their dusty attics to your clean nursery. Again, be sure to safety-check all borrowed or donated cribs.

Replace cribs with playpens (or bassinets for newborns). The new playpens (also known as play yards) are much cheaper and more convenient than cribs. Both playpens and bassinets can easily be moved from room to room as needed. You'll find safety checklists for playpens and bassinets on page 40.

Eliminate cribs from your nursery. If you can't afford to invest in safe cribs or playpens, don't have cribs at all. In my nursery experience, I've encountered very few babies—and not a single toddler— who make a regular habit of sleeping in the church nursery. Micah certainly never did. Those who do are often newborns who are just as happy (or even happier) sleeping in their infant carriers or snuggling up on a loving caregiver's shoulder. So instead of stocking up on extra cribs, recruit extra sets of arms.

Will parents notice the missing cribs? Maybe. But their concerns will melt away when you explain that in your church, nursery workers hold and love the babies rather than leaving them alone in cribs.

Once you've safety-checked and removed or replaced cribs as

necessary, you may want to post a copy of the "Crib Safety Checklist" (p. 39) in your room to let parents know that all the cribs in your nursery (whether new or used) are safe.

Setting Up Cribs for Safe and Peaceful Slumber

Now that you've obtained "safe-looking" cribs, you'll want to make them cozy and inviting. Cover firm, snug-fitting crib mattresses with cotton or flannel crib sheets. Crib bumpers add an extra home-like touch to your nursery and cushion bumps for early rollers. (Don't put bumpers in cribs that will be used by older babies who could become entangled in them.) You can purchase crib linens in any baby or department store, but if you ask around, parents probably have more than a few to spare. Baby fabrics and patterns are also available if you have willing seamstresses in your congregation.

In addition to sheets and bumpers, gather receiving blankets. Small, lightweight blankets are best. Avoid soft bedding such as pillows, comforters, and sheepskins that could suffocate babies. If your church doesn't already have a collection of receiving blankets, donations are your best bet. Receiving blankets are useful for infant floor-play and sleeping—they can be used to play Peekaboo and other games with older babies and toddlers.

 **NURSERY NOTE**

How many cribs should you have in your nursery? That depends on how many babies you care for and how much space you have available. In general, your sleeping area should take up no more than a third of your total room space.

If you're concerned about space, you may want to look into stacking crib units. But be prepared. Although stacking units save space, they may initially draw some criticism from parents—these cribs really do put babies "behind bars." Angie Shelton of Grace Community Church in Tyler, Texas, recently added stacking crib units to her church's small nursery. She said, "Many people were against the idea because of their cagelike appearance, but we had no choice. It was either stacking cribs or no floorspace for the babies to play. Now that we have them, everyone is thrilled with them."

The younger the babies, the more likely they are to sleep. So if you have a newborn room, you'll want to provide several cribs if space and resources allow. Since toddlers spend most of their time playing, their rooms probably don't even need cribs (if you have regular toddler sleepers, consider providing mats).

Create a peaceful environment for sleeping babies by placing your cozy cribs in a separate section of the room (or an adjacent room if one is available). For safety reasons, you should place cribs away from windows, draperies, or blinds. Avoid placing cribs near doors, supply cabinets, or other high-traffic areas. If older babies and toddlers are present, help them play and talk quietly so babies can sleep.

As infants wake from their peaceful slumber, they'll enjoy looking at and interacting with crib toys such as mobiles or busy boxes. Black-and-white images or bright, contrasting colors work best for babies' still-developing vision. Musical mobiles can help soothe crying babies. Remove mobiles and dangling toys from cribs that will be used by babies five months or older.

CPSC recommends that all crib toys meet the following safety standards:

- no strings with loops or openings having perimeters greater than fourteen inches,
- no strings or cords longer than seven inches that dangle into the crib, and
- no components small enough to be a choking hazard (smaller than a fifty-cent piece).

Changing Tables and Other Diapering Doodads

Waah! Just when you thought your nursery had descended into safe and peaceful slumber, a baby wakes up. And another. And another. How will you handle them now? With rubber gloves and baby wipes and diaper pails all in a row.

You should change babies' diapers at least once each nursery session (and more frequently if diapers are soiled). And the best place to change a diaper is on a sturdy diaper-changing table.

The CPSC recommends changing tables that provide easily accessible shelves or drawers to store diapers, wipes, and other diaper-changing paraphernalia. But more importantly, CPSC-approved changing tables will also be equipped with safety straps to prevent falls. Always use safety straps, and **never, never leave a baby on a changing table unattended.**

If changing tables aren't available, consider using a wide countertop—but only if you're sure workers will always keep at least one hand on babies as they're being changed. Otherwise, change babies on a pad on the floor where falls won't be an issue. Don't change babies in cribs that other children will use later.

Ideally, your diaper-changing area should be set up near a sink and should be equipped with the following supplies (if your room isn't equipped with a sink, workers will need to wash their hands in the restroom after each diaper change):

- a washable or disposable pad;
- extra disposable diapers in appropriate sizes;
- baby wipes;
- disposable rubber gloves;
- a childproof wastebasket lined with a disposable liner;
- disposable bags (for soiled diapers, gloves, and wipes); and
- disinfectant (to clean the pad after each diaper change).

Make sure diaper-changing supplies and wastebaskets are inaccessible to children.

The Swing Shift: How to Choose and Use Swings and Other Equipment

Swings, walkers, and other optional equipment can provide added variety for babies and relief for workers' weary arms. As with any equipment, check each item carefully for safety. Provide adequate supervision: Swings, activity seats, Exersaucers, and especially walkers aren't baby sitters. Babies need constant, watchful care.

With those general safety cautions in mind, you may want to consider buying or acquiring the following baby equipment:

Swings—Baby swings have a seemingly miraculous way of calming fussy infants—and sometimes even lulling them to sleep. A swing also can provide a safe place for you to set down one baby while tending to another. Some new swings even have open tops to make it easier to get babies in and out safely. Swings are available in battery-operated or wind-up models. Since wind-up models only run for up to fifteen minutes at a time, many parents today opt to purchase the slightly more expensive battery-operated swings. However, in a nursery setting with multiple babies, activities, and caregivers, a fifteen-minute "swing time" per baby is probably more than adequate.

Unlike used cribs, used swings can generally be considered safe as long as they're stable and in good condition with a functioning safety strap. Always strap babies into the swings, and limit their use to babies under twenty-five pounds (unless the owner's manual lists a higher weight limit).

Activity seats—Also known as bouncy seats or infant seats, the activity seat is to baby what a recliner is to Mom and Dad—a place to sit back, relax, and enjoy the company. Activity seats hold babies in a semi-upright position and provide them with a better view of their surroundings. Many of these seats also provide toys ("activities") to entertain babies. As with swings, always fasten baby into the seat, and observe the recommended twenty-five-pound weight limit.

Walkers or Exersaucers—Remember "Nanelcam's" comment, "they used walkers (!) and old ones at that." Why all the fuss about walkers?

Even with supervision, walkers really aren't safe. Baby walkers cause more injuries to children under five than any other baby furniture product (Ann Brown, "Consumer News," Good Housekeeping, June 1995). The American Academy of Pediatrics has recommended that baby walkers be banned ("Injuries Associated with Infant Walkers," Pediatrics, May 1995). Walkers allow nonwalking babies to "walk" into walls, out of doors, down stairs, and right into all sorts of trouble. When used too early and too often, they can also damage babies' developing feet.

A better alternative is the Exersaucer (manufactured by EvenFlo) or a stationary activity center (available through several other baby companies). Babies can stand, sit, rock, bounce, and play with attached toys without "walking" into dangerous places. Stationary activity centers have only been available for a few years, so any used ones you acquire will probably be safe and in good condition. And since they don't come apart for storage, Exersaucers are another item that parents of walking toddlers or preschoolers would likely be thrilled to loan out.

Child-sized tables and chairs—"Children want big chairs if they're available," said Mary Davis of New Testament Christian Church in Keokuk, Iowa. But big chairs can cause big spills for little ones. So Mary has no adult chairs in her nursery—grown-ups crawl around on the floor right along with the babies.

For toddler rooms, sturdy child-sized furniture can come in handy. A child-sized table provides a work surface for coloring, sculpting with modeling dough, or playing with sand and water. If you're on a limited budget, buy a table and skip the chairs—most toddlers aren't likely to sit in them for very long anyway.

High chairs—Although you aren't likely to serve many baby meals in the nursery, your nursery department can serve the church by acquiring one or two high chairs for use at church dinners, moms' luncheons, and other food-related functions. Safety checklists for high chairs and hook-on seats are on page 41.

Gates—If your nursery includes adjoining rooms, you may want to use safety gates. Gates can keep wandering toddlers from running into creeping or sleeping areas used by younger babies. And if your nursery doesn't have a split door, gates can provide a way for parents to retrieve their children without releasing the whole herd. Never install gates on outside doors that must be used as fire exits.

Parents magazine offers the following advice for selecting and using safety gates:

- A gate should be at least thirty-two inches high to keep toddlers from climbing over it.
- Any gate openings should be no more than 2⅜ inches wide.
- A gate should stand securely in place. Hardware-mounted gates should be anchored to walls.
- Expanding bars on a pressure gate should be on the side opposite the children to prevent pinched fingers.
- Rubber end caps on a pressure gate should be checked and cleaned frequently. Dirty caps don't grip well.
- An accordion-style gate, which can easily trap a child's head in its wide openings, should never be used.

Also according to Parents magazine, in 1994, safety gates caused nearly 1,200 injuries to children aged four and younger. (Ironically, these gates were probably installed by parents hoping to prevent injuries!) By choosing the right type of gate—and installing it properly—you'll be able to prevent rather than provoke injuries.

Grown-Up Gear

Babies aren't the only regular visitors to your church nursery. From time to time, volunteers, parents, and other grown-ups may

---

NURSERY NOTE

Shopping for rocking chairs? According to Tammy Ross, the director of preschool ministries at First Baptist Church in Columbia, Tennessee, the new glider-rockers are a big improvement over regular rocking chairs. "Regular rockers 'rock' into the beds, walls, and the middle of the room," Tammy said. "They also pose a hazard to tiny fingers. Gliders are so much better and more comfortable. They stay in one place and glide so easily!" Tammy recommended checking with local furniture stores for special deals on gliders. At one hundred fifty dollars to two hundred dollars, they're a substantial, but worthwhile, investment.

choose to visit Baby Central. The following items will make them (and their stuff) feel at home in the nursery.

Rocking chairs—A comfortable rocking chair is a must for an infant nursery. In addition to adding yet another home-like touch, it helps nursery volunteers rest and work at the same time. When placed behind a privacy screen or in a separate room, rocking chairs also provide a peaceful haven for nursing mothers.

Shelves or cabinets—You'll need a place to store name tags, sign-in sheets, bulletin board and teaching materials, and other grown-up stuff. If cabinets are at ground level, install locks or safety latches to keep out curious creepers.

Diaper bag depositories—Babies' bags and workers' packs and purses should be stored out of children's reach. If your nursery facility doesn't have built-in cubbies for diaper-bag storage, install diaper-bag hooks on the wall out of children's reach. For regular attendees, you may even want to label your hooks or cubbies to help parents and workers locate diaper bags quickly.

Your once-bare nursery room is fast approaching baby-zone status. It's clean, it's safe, and it's filled with all the right equipment. Almost. Add a good selection of age-appropriate toys, and your nursery will really come to life.

CRIB SAFETY CHECKLIST

Before you place a crib in your church nursery, make sure you can mark "yes" for the following statements.

_____ 1. I have measured the slat spacing. Slats are spaced no more than 2⅜ inches apart.

_____ 2. I have checked to see that no slats are missing or cracked.

_____ 3. I have checked to see that the mattress fits snugly. There is less than two-fingers width between the edge of the mattress and the crib side.

_____ 4. I have checked to see that the mattress support is securely attached to the headboard and footboard.

_____ 5. I have measured the corner posts, if present. Corner posts are no higher than 1/16 inch to prevent entanglement of clothing or other objects worn by children.

_____ 6. I have made sure there are no cutouts in the headboards and footboards that allow head entrapment.

_____ 7. I have checked to see that the drop-side latches cannot be easily released by babies.

_____ 8. I have checked to see that the drop-side latches securely hold crib sides in the raised position.

_____ 9. I have checked to see that all screws or bolts which secure crib components are present and tight.

_____ 10. I have checked to see that any paint used on cribs is lead-free.

PLAYPEN AND BASSINET SAFETY CHECKLIST

Before you place a playpen or bassinet in your church nursery, make sure you can mark "yes" for the following statements.

Playpens

_____ 1. I have checked to see that drop-side mesh playpens have warning labels never to leave the side in the down position.

_____ 2. I have checked to see that the mesh has a fine weave that won't catch on clothing buttons or allow little fingers to slip through.

_____ 3. I have checked to see that the mesh has no tears, holes, or loose threads.

_____ 4. I have checked to see that the mesh is securely attached to the top rail and floor plate.

_____ 5. I have checked to see that the top rail cover has no tears or holes.

_____ 6. I have checked to see that wooden playpen slats are spaced no more than two inches apart.

_____ 7. I have checked to see that any staples used in construction are firmly installed and none are missing or loose.

Bassinets

_____ 1. I have checked to see that the bassinet has a sturdy bottom and wide base for stability.

_____ 2. I have checked to see that the bassinet has smooth surfaces with no protruding staples or hardware that might injure babies.

_____ 3. I have checked to see that the legs have strong, effective locks to prevent folding while in use.

_____ 4. I have checked to see that the mattress is firm and snugly fitted.

HIGH CHAIR AND HOOK-ON SEAT SAFETY CHECKLIST

Before you acquire high chairs or hook-on seats for your church, check for the following safety features. Never leave children unattended in high chairs or hook-on seats. And always use high chair restraining straps to prevent babies from sliding under the tray and strangling.

High Chairs

_____ 1. The high chair has waist and crotch restraining straps that are independent of the tray.

_____ 2. The high chair tray locks securely.

_____ 3. The buckle on the waist strap is easy to use.

_____ 4. The high chair has a wide, stable base.

_____ 5. Tubing caps or plugs are firmly attached and cannot be pulled off and swallowed by a child.

_____ 6. The folding high chair has an effective locking device to keep the chair from collapsing.

Hook-On Chairs

_____ 1. The hook-on chair has a restraining strap to secure the child.

_____ 2. The hook-on chair has a clamp that locks onto the table for added security.

_____ 3. Tubing caps or plugs are firmly attached and cannot be pulled off and swallowed by a child.

_____ 4. The hook-on chair has a warning never to place the chair where the child can push off with feet.

BUSY HANDS, BUSY FEET

Selecting the best toys for your nursery

"I once had the opportunity to care for children in a church nursery. In the beginning, it was awful! There were not enough toys to go around or to keep the kids interested...I brought books, which the kids loved. I brought tambourines and sand blocks and triangles and toy plastic flutes and we all made a joyful noise unto the Lord... After that, things were great!"

"GRANDMA"
FROM AMERICA ONLINE

Before I became a parent, I knew two classes of toys. There were big-kid toys like Legos, Barbies, bikes, and toy trucks. And there were baby toys like rattles, mobiles, and stacking rings. Now that I'm a mom, I know there are probably two thousand classes of baby toys alone. There are crib toys and stroller toys, car seat toys and high chair toys. And more teething toys than you can shake a rattle at.

Does your baby—or your nursery—really need all these things? Absolutely not. In fact, the Oppenheim Toy Portfolio's *Best Toys, Books, Videos & Software for Kids, 1997* infant toy section includes this disclaimer: "No baby needs all the toys listed here" (Joanne and Stephanie Oppenheim). And they're right. No amount of toys can replace the attention of a caring, loving parent or nursery worker. But after I recovered from the shocking realization of the sheer number of baby toys available, I had another revelation—this one much more gradually.

Currently, I juggle the responsibilities of mom, freelance writer, volunteer nursery coordinator, and Christian educator, and I do most of my work from home. While I type, Micah plays with toys, usually in his crib. Six months of work and several lengthy bouts of crying later, I've realized the importance of toy selection. Age-appropriate toys make a big difference. And for babies, age is measured in months, not years. To keep Micah entertained, I've learned to shop carefully for toys that engage and challenge him at each developmental stage.

All baby toys aren't created equal. The perfect toy for an infant will be ignored by six months, refused by nine months, and put away by a year. The toy suggestions on pages 43-50 will help you select toys and books that will keep babies (and workers) of all ages happily entertained when they visit your nursery.

pages 43-50

Here Today, Gone Tomorrow: Toys for Newborns

With Micah not yet two, many of our infant toys have already farmed themselves out to new homes. Rattles and teethers simply don't hold the attention of older babies and toddlers. "So it shakes," they seem to think. "Big deal. Can't it do anything else?"

That's the bad news. The good news is that infant toys seldom wear out. So you may be able to acquire most of your infant toys from parents of toddlers. More good news: In most churches, new babies are ready to use the toys by the time older babies have outgrown the toys. If you choose your infant toys carefully, they should last for several years.

Infants need specific kinds of toys, but they don't need a lot of toys. The following list will get you started.

Mirrors—A variety of baby-safe mirrors are available. Some are designed to hang in cribs and may have high-contrast illustrations on the reverse side. Other baby mirrors are free-standing for floor play. Baby mirrors may also be found in activity centers, where they're often combined with rattles, spinners, or squeakers. For safety purposes, you should only use crib mirrors and activity centers in cribs with babies five months or younger.

Mobiles—Baby stores are flooded with mobiles—and for good reason. Mobiles bring dangling objects within babies' range of vision (usually eight to fourteen inches). Mobiles can also add a nice finishing touch to your nursery décor. When selecting a mobile, however, décor should take a back seat to baby-friendliness. In order for a baby to really see the mobile, the dangling items need to face downward. In other words, any critters dangling from your mobile should be standing on their heads!

Musical toys—Babies love to hear soothing music, and today's musical toys are much lighter (and safer for babies) than their predecessors. Instead of heavy music boxes with metal wind-up keys, many musical toys come in soft, plush figures with pull-down activation. There are giraffes with pull-down necks, flowers with pull-down stems, and a whole horde of other cuddly crooners. Remove musical toys from cribs used by rolling or sitting babies to avoid suffocation.

Rattles—Rattles to be used by infants should be soft enough for babies to grab. Like musical toys, many of today's rattles have their shakers housed in friendly animal faces. Avoid loud rattles that may startle or scare babies. Reserve heavier plastic or wooden rattles for older babies, or have workers shake the rattles as they hold and play with infants. Make sure all rattles are constructed in one piece and are large enough so they can't enter and become lodged in an infant's throat.

Activity centers—Infants three months and older will enjoy lying on an activity quilt or gazing up and batting at an activity gym. Some activity gyms are designed to be mounted in cribs; others are free-standing or attached to a floor mat. All types encourage development of hand-eye coordination.

Books—Infants are perfect listeners. They can touch and feel soft books, but they can't yet reach out and tear up paper books. Providing books in your infant nursery also gives workers an easy opportunity to talk to the babies. Some nursery workers may be new parents with high "coo" quotients, but for others, talking to a seemingly unresponsive baby may feel unnatural. And current research has shown that talking to babies early and often fosters healthy language development in the toddler and preschool years.

Sitting Pretty: Toys for Older Babies

Babies who can sit, scoot, and crawl are ready for a wider selection of toys. In addition to the toys listed above, you'll want to add playthings from the following categories.

Age-appropriate rattles and teethers—Older babies are ready for bigger rattles and other manipulatives they can use in two-handed play. Look for items that offer a variety of textures and shapes. And since teeth can begin to poke through as early as four months, it's a good idea to provide little ones with safe toys to chew on. (Clean toys before they get passed from mouth to mouth. See pages 53-55 for more information on toy cleaning.)

Blocks—Block play strengthens babies' developing large and small muscles. Babies love blocks, but they don't play with blocks the same way preschoolers and older children do. For older babies, few games are more fun than filling and dumping a container of small plastic blocks. Most babies also enjoy holding, carrying, or pushing larger blocks around. A few babies might even attempt to place the blocks in rows or stacks. But don't expect to see babies building block buildings.

Blocks for babies should be lightweight plastic, fabric, or cardboard. Avoid the hard wooden blocks used by older children; they're too heavy for babies to carry and can cause injuries when dropped on unsuspecting nursery mates. Place blocks in an open, low-traffic area that's visible from other parts of the room.

NURSERY NOTE

Can't afford to buy soft blocks? In *Love, Laughter, and Learning,* Melinda Mahand and Clara Mae Van Brink suggest an easy way to make your own. Simply collect clean and dry pint, quart, and half-gallon cardboard milk cartons. Stuff the cartons with newspaper; then flatten the pointed ends and fold and tape the cartons shut. If you want color, cover each block with colored contact paper.

Other block variations include linking loops or snap beads. The ever-popular Lego and Duplo blocks are also now available for babies. Recommended for ages six months and up, Duplo baby blocks have soft edges and rounded bumps that are easy for little hands to fit together. Some sets include rattle blocks, animal figures, and wheeled cars.

Rolling toys—Soft cars, balls, and other rolling toys will encourage babies to practice their developing mobility. Look for soft fabric or plastic toys that are large enough for babies to handle with both hands. Avoid foam or Nerf toys. Although these toys are soft, the foam can easily tear and find its way into babies' mouths.

Before they know it (and often before you know it!), babies in pursuit of a rolling toy have propelled themselves across the entire room. Rolling toys also provide opportunities for workers to interact with babies as they demonstrate, "See how it rolls. Can you roll it?"

Plush pals—Fuzzy animals and friendly dolls make great playmates for babies on the move. Babies will enjoy hugging and kissing plush pals, playing Peekaboo with furry friends, or simply dragging the stuffed figures around with them. The Oppenheim Toy Portfolio recommends the following features when shopping for baby-friendly plush toys:

- interesting textures,
- easy-to-grasp legs or arms,
- sound effects sewn safely inside,
- washable fabrics such as velour or terry cloth,
- stitched-on features (no loose ribbons or bells), and
- size small enough for infant to hold with ease.

Action toys—Floor toys that pop up, squeak, spin, or rattle are sure to be big hits with older babies. I don't think I've visited a nursery yet that didn't have at least one pop-up surprise box. These inexpensive, interactive toys have been around for years; babies push a button, turn a dial, or move a lever, and up pops a smiling friend. Best of all, these toys grow with babies. At first babies enjoy the pop-up surprises with the help of an adult. Then they learn to shut the doors. Before long, they're operating buttons, then levers, and can enjoy playing with the toy independently.

Toy Safety for Infants and Babies

According to the Oppenheim Toy Portfolio, you should avoid the following toys, which can pose choking or suffocation hazards for infants and babies:

- antique rattles;
- foam toys;

- toys with elastic;
- toys with buttons, bells, and ribbons;
- old wooden toys that may contain lead paint;
- furry plush dolls that shed; and
- any toys with small parts.

Play, Puzzles, and Pretend: Toys for Toddlers and Twos

Toddlers and twos sometimes seem like miniature perpetual-motion machines. They walk or run about, flitting from toy to toy, hovering only until the next new challenge comes into view. These little active learners need a variety of toys to match their growing abilities. Toys for quiet times, run-about times, independent play, and side-by-side play should find their way into your toddler toy collection. Here are some good choices to get you started.

Push toys—Wheeled push toys allow beginning walkers—and even cruisers—to venture out on their own. The familiar corn popper is still a favorite, but countless other choices are also available. You can find lawn mowers, shopping carts, cars, wagons, and even a working dump truck. Look for toys that are sturdy, stable, and sized for toddlers. Avoid larger, pedaled toys intended for preschoolers.

Pull toys—Sturdy walkers who are able to walk while looking over their shoulders will enjoy pulling a toy along as they play. From ducks and dogs to trains and planes, pull toys are available for every budget. You can even make your own by firmly attaching strings to decorated shoe boxes. For safety reasons, pull toys should have strings no longer than twelve inches.

Toy phones—Babies love phones. Like their grown-up counterparts, toy phones are available in a variety of styles and colors. Most toy phones make ringing, beeping, or buzzing sounds, and some even feature voice messages. Avoid letting babies play with real phones that have dangerous cords and wires.

Toy vehicles—Vrroom! Vrroom! Two-year-olds love to "drive" toy cars. While younger toddlers may not yet be aspiring race-car drivers, they do enjoy pushing around toy buses, trains, cars, and trucks. Large toy trucks can even carry important cargo such as blocks, books, or small toys.

Plush pals—Toddlers will continue to enjoy playing with dolls and stuffed animals. They delight in carrying soft, floppy companions with them on their explorations. Older toddlers may begin to be interested in dressing (and undressing!) dolls with removable clothes. This is also a good time to introduce dolls with zippers, buttons (large and tightly sewn on), and buckles. Because toddlers still put things in their mouths, you'll want to avoid dolls with long hair and animals with thick fur.

Musical toys—Push-a-button, make-a-sound toys help toddlers learn about cause and effect. Animal sounds, traffic sounds, and simple songs are available in addition to the traditional squeakers and beepers. Toddlers will also enjoy using shakers and other simple rhythm instruments. You can easily make your own rhythm instruments with household objects such as film canisters and oatmeal containers. Just add a few dry beans, firmly tape or hot-glue the lids shut, and you've got an instant maraca band.

Climbing toys—Slides, tunnels, or vinyl-covered foam cubes make great exploratoriums for little climbers. Bright, sturdy plastic slides and climbers are veritable toddler magnets, but most require an investment of fifty dollars or more. For a cheaper alternative, set up a climbing area with a mountain of firm pillows. In either case, always supervise toddlers as they climb.

Ride-on toys—Vehicle push toys such as cars, trucks, and trains can find new life as ride-ons. (I can only imagine the chaos that will envelop our house when Micah's feet touch the ground on his push train!) A variety of pedalless plastic cars and trucks are also available. If your room is small, you may want to save these large, moving toys for outside play.

Toys for pretend play—Every time Micah sees me cooking at the stove, he says, "Stir, stir, stir." Toddlers love toys that allow them to do what they see grown-ups doing. If your room doesn't have a housekeeping or home-living center, by all means set one up!

First, decide what kind of investment you want to make. Keep in mind that the equipment you provide will get used again and again, so it should be sturdy. Toddlers are perfectly happy with homemade moving-box "appliances," but if you choose to go this route, you may find yourself "remodeling" your kitchen more often than you'd like. You can obtain a long-lasting, wooden kitchen center for less than two hundred dollars and a slightly less durable, much less expensive plastic version for as little as thirty-five dollars.

To outfit your kitchen, buy play dishes or bring in items from home. Avoid fake food that toddlers may try to eat. The following home kitchen items are generally toddler-friendly:

- small, lightweight pots and pans;
- margarine or yogurt containers with lids;
- empty cereal boxes;
- empty milk cartons (clean and dry);
- empty dish-soap bottles (clean and dry);
- short-handled wooden spoons (sanded if the wood was rough);
- plastic cups, bowls, or plates;
- measuring cups (not glass); and
- plastic or wooden spatulas.

Play settings with miniature-people toys also encourage pretend play. (Be sure miniature-people toys aren't small enough to be choking hazards. Fisher-Price Little People made before 1991 should not be used by children under age three.) Available play settings include houses, garages, farms, and playgrounds.

Art supplies—Older toddlers are ready to venture into the world of art. At this age, art projects are for touching and feeling and experimenting, not for creating a finely finished product. Modeling dough is a great art medium for tactile exploration and is easy to make yourself. Just combine one cup of flour and one-half cup of salt with a little cooking oil and enough water to make a smooth dough. (For colored dough, mix food coloring with the water before adding it to the dough.) Knead the dough, and then store it in an airtight container. Supervise toddlers closely as they work with modeling dough, and remind them often that the dough is for playing—not eating.

Toddlers also enjoy coloring with large, chubby crayons and "painting" with water and large paintbrushes.

Simple puzzles—To a toddler, a shape sorter is a puzzle. A set of stacking and nesting cups is a puzzle. Putting aerosol can lids in a muffin tin is a puzzle. Stick to puzzles with no more than six pieces. Each piece should depict an entire object. For example, an appropriate farm puzzle for toddlers might have a cow piece, a pig piece, a barn piece, and a farmer piece. This design is much more toddler-friendly than a farm puzzle with four pieces that form one cow.

Lightweight balls—Playing with balls helps toddlers exercise their developing large muscles. Most toddlers enjoy throwing or rolling balls to a willing partner. Choose large, lightweight balls that toddlers can easily grasp. Soft fabric balls or slightly deflated beach balls work best.

Books—In *Love, Laughter, and Learning,* Melinda Mahand and Clara Mae Van Brink point out that books are valuable for young children's mental, physical, social, and spiritual growth. Mahand and Van

Brink list these and other ways books can benefit children. Books...

- help children learn to think.
- develop hand-eye coordination and large and small muscles as children carry books, turn pages, and point to pictures.
- help children identify and understand emotions.
- increase children's awareness of the world God made.
- provide opportunities for children to hear Bible stories and see Bible-story pictures.
- help children develop an understanding of how to work and live with others the way the Bible teaches us to live.

What kinds of books are best for toddlers? Simple Bible-story books; books about the world around them; simple stories about babies and their families; picture books with animals, colors, or numbers—just about any children's book that holds their attention! Toddlers also love lift-the-flap books (less complicated, sturdier versions of the pop-up books older children enjoy). They can sit through longer stories and may ask for you to repeat the same book again and again. Some toddlers I've worked with (including my own) have even memorized favorite books.

Toy Safety for Toddlers and Twos

According to the Oppenheim Toy Portfolio, avoid the following toys, which can pose choking or suffocation hazards for toddlers and twos:

- foam toys;
- toys with small parts (including small plastic fake foods);
- dolls and stuffed animals with fuzzy or long hair;
- toys labeled "three and up" (this label usually indicates that there are small parts in or on the toy); and
- latex balloons (according to CPSC, more than one hundred ten children have died from suffocation involving uninflated balloons or pieces of broken balloons since 1973!).

Let's Go Shopping...in the Sanctuary?

So many toys, so little time. Or money. If you're wondering how on earth you'll ever be able to acquire all this stuff, take heart. Here's how three churches got their congregations excited about outfitting their nurseries.

Although they share the same name, the First Baptist Church in Columbia, Tennessee, and the First Baptist Church in Decatur, Georgia, are hundreds of miles apart. And both are across the country from Overlake Christian Church in Kirkland, Washington. But all three churches have used the same idea for acquiring nursery and toddler-room toys—and all have had great success.

At Overlake, Linda Byram needed more toys to fill the nursery in the church's new building. So she and her workers announced a nursery shower. They cut out catalog pictures of baby items (toys and other equipment), glued the pictures to paper teddy bears, and posted them on a bulletin board. Church members took home the bears and brought back the toys. Donations ranged from books and rattles to swings and Exersaucers.

Barbara Long, minister of childhood education at First Baptist, Decatur, was so optimistic about the toy shower idea that she bought all the toy items in advance. In her small community, many store owners were willing to lend out things on commission—to be paid for or returned after the shower. She and her workers set out the price-labeled books and toys on a Sunday morning, along with coffee and doughnuts. "We spent fifteen hundred dollars to two thousand dollars," said Barbara, "and we sold all but three hundred dollars. I somehow found the money in my budget to buy the rest." For first-time showers, Barbara recommended choosing a date and time when people would normally be at church (Sunday morning before services works well, as does the time before or after a well-attended midweek program).

First Baptist, Columbia, has held toy showers for the past four years in conjunction with an annual Preschool Ministry Open House. Like Barbara Long, director of preschool ministries Tammy Ross purchased needed items ahead of time with the agreement that they would be returned if the money wasn't raised. Tammy has never had to return anything over the four years and has raised thousands of dollars through her efforts. Tammy said that after four years, her church's collection of age-appropriate toys,

NURSERY NOTE

TOY EXTRA: MAKING YOUR OWN TOYS

Homemade toys can replace or supplement the toys listed here. For ideas, check out *Love, Laughter, and Learning* (Mahand and Van Brink, Convention Press, 1996); *Infants & Toddlers: Curriculum and Teaching* (LaVisa Cam Wilson, Delmar Publishers Inc., 1990); or *More Things to Do with Toddlers and Twos* (Karen Miller, TelShare Publishing, Inc., 1990).

equipment, and books has improved. They now have a good selection of items that are in good condition.

At Tammy's church, the Preschool Ministry Open House lasts from four to six weeks. Each week, Tammy displays needed items in the hallway between the church's nursery and preschool areas. Church members can purchase specific items or donate money toward the overall goal. The open house also allows parents and other church members to see the nursery and preschool facilities.

Sounds like a great idea, you think, but our church could never raise that much money. Maybe not, but maybe you don't need to. The substantial fund-raising efforts of First Baptist, Columbia, reflect the length of the open house program and the size of the congregation—seven hundred to eight hundred members with around one hundred fifty preschoolers attending each week. A smaller church will have fewer resources but will also have smaller needs. Toys for twenty cost much less than toys for two hundred.

So what are you waiting for? Start dreaming...then go shopping.

RUB-A-DUB SCRUB

Keeping toys and equipment clean and sanitary

"Our toys, beds, and equipment are washed and disinfected after each session! This has resulted in a much cleaner nursery and healthier babies. Our toys last much longer also as a result of good cleaning and upkeep."

TAMMY ROSS
COLUMBIA, TENNESSEE

N o parent wants to leave a child in a nursery with dirty toys. Or dirty cribs. Or dirty floors. But as I talked with nursery directors, I was surprised to find out how many churches don't make nursery cleaning a priority. "We have a system, but I'm not sure how effective it is," said one nursery director. "The workers are supposed to clean the toys after each service, but I usually have to go in and check afterward," reported another. Very few churches I talked with—even large ones—have a working cleanup system in place.

At Tammy Ross' church, all toys and equipment used by children are washed and disinfected after each session. In addition, the church custodian vacuums and/or mops the rooms every day. Every six months, all the furniture is moved out and the rooms are professionally cleaned. "Preschoolers are on or close to the floor constantly," Tammy said. "The church's nursery should be the cleanest room in the building."

While no church is likely to dispute Tammy's claim, churches all around the country seem to have a hard time mustering up cleaning crews and equipment to get the job done. So I asked Tammy Ross to share the secrets to her cleaning success. As I suspected, First Baptist's cleaning system started small. Very small. With Tammy Ross.

"I did most of it myself at first," said Tammy. "I just stayed after services and made sure everything was clean before I left." Your workers will only take their commitment to cleanliness as seriously as you do. When you make a commitment to maintaining a clean, healthy nursery environment, others will eventually join you. When Tammy stayed long enough for early arriving Sunday-evening nursery workers to notice, they volunteered to help. Now they help on a regular basis. With three people working together, the nursery is cleaned and disinfected in no time.

Nursery cleanup doesn't have to be a dreadful chore. Just round up a few volunteers, pop in your favorite Christian music, and enjoy some good fellowship while you work. A thorough nursery cleaning should include (at minimum) the following four tasks:

1. All equipment surfaces should be wiped down with bleach solution (one part bleach to ten parts water), and equipment should be returned to its proper place.

2. Clean linens should be placed in all cribs, playpens, or bassinets. Wondering which linens need changing? *The Nurturing Nursery* (Debbie Paschang, et al.) suggests having workers place a folded receiving blanket on top of each clean bed. If the blanket is missing or crumpled, the bed needs to be changed.

3. All plastic toys should be soaked in bleach solution, air-dried, and then put away. In Children's Ministry Magazine (May/June 1995), Michelle Maris suggested using a two-tub disinfecting method. Fill one tub with bleach solution and a second tub with hot rinse water. Submerge toys in the bleach solution for at least thirty seconds, and then give the toys a good rinse before allowing them to air dry.

4. Carpets should be vacuumed; floors should be swept and mopped.

Do you really have to wash every single toy every single time? Only if you aren't sure which toys have been used. At Eugene

NURSERY NOTE

Nursery workers disagree about the use and cleaning of plush toys. You can clean dusty stuffed animals by sprinkling them with baking soda and then vigorously brushing each toy. But they can't be sanitized with bleach solution the way plastic toys can. For this reason, First Baptist Church (Columbia, Tennessee) doesn't keep plush toys in their nursery or preschool classrooms. Eugene Christian Fellowship (Eugene, Oregon) keeps plush toys in separate bins. With a washer and dryer on-site, it's easy to launder the toys with the crib linens. For best results, stick to plush toys with washable fabrics such as velour or terry cloth.

Christian Fellowship (ECF) in Eugene, Oregon, one worker in each service is in charge of watching for toys that find their way into children's mouths. Before the toys pass their germs along to other children, toys are whisked away into the sink and disinfected before the next service. ECF also keeps a separate tub of toys for each service; that way if the check-in-check-out time between services is too hectic for disinfecting, clean toys are still available. Tammy Ross' church maintains a large "Dirty Toys" bin for toys waiting to be cleaned. Because some preschool rooms don't have sinks, each classroom has a spray bottle of bleach solution for on-the-spot cleaning.

Dirty toys must be cleaned before they're used again. Unused toys don't have to be disinfected every time, but they should be cleaned and inspected at least once a month to ensure general safety and cleanliness. When you inspect toys, check plastic toys for breakage or loose parts. Check wooden toys for sharp or splintered edges. Any toys that are inspected and found to be broken or damaged should be replaced or repaired immediately.

You can store clean toys on shelves or in cupboards or safe toy boxes. Barbara Curtis is a big supporter of toy shelves. In her home, toys for her children of all ages are stored in clear plastic bins on labeled shelves. To make cleanup easier for young children, you can label bins and shelves with matching pictures.

If you choose to store toys in toy boxes or toy chests, the CPSC recommends toy chests that have lids that will stay open in any position and will not fall unexpectedly on a child. Avoid toy boxes with sharp edges that could cut or hinges that could pinch or squeeze little fingers. For extra safety, look for lids with ventilation holes just in case a child decides to climb inside. Whatever toy storage method you choose, help children put their toys safely away after playing so children won't step on or trip over their toys.

After all the time you've spent cleaning, maintaining, and storing toys, you'll want to do everything you can to keep them that way. By controlling access to your nursery, you'll ensure that your hard work wasn't all for naught.

CLOSING THE REVOLVING DOOR

Controlling access to the nursery

*"We're beginning to lock up toys and sup-
plies to prevent theft or misplaced items."*

CONNIE SYLVESTER
CHARLOTTESVILLE, VIRGINIA

I originally had planned to visit Christ Community Church on a
Friday afternoon. When my flight was delayed by bad weather,
nursery coordinator Connie Sylvester and I ended up meeting
Sunday morning. Since services were going on, the nursery had the
only empty seats available—a unique opportunity to compare a
church's nursery theory with its practice.

Except for Micah coming over to check on me every few minutes,
most of the toddlers didn't even notice us. The teen helper seemed
somewhat interested in our conversation, but the teacher merrily
went about her business as she helped the children build a church
out of blocks. Early in our session, a volunteer from another classroom popped in. "Does your room have a tape player?" he asked the
teacher with a panicked look on his face. "Mine's missing."

Connie (who had just finished explaining how the nursery facilities
were used for weddings, Bible studies, counseling sessions, and other
church functions) paused for a moment to assist in the equipment
transfer and then returned. That was when she told me about the plans
for new locking cabinets for toys and other supplies. Like tape players.

I can relate to the missing tape-player caper because when I teach
in the early childhood department, I usually bring my own. I know the
church has a tape player (and probably more than one), but as a volunteer, I'm never quite sure which room it's supposed to "live" in.
Although tape players may be borrowed by other children's or adult
Sunday school classes, most nursery-specific supplies are unlikely to
wander off to new homes in your church. When was the last time the

youth group borrowed your diaper pail?

But at Christ Community Church, up to eighteen different workers pass through the early childhood area on a given Sunday morning. At Scottsdale Bible Church, it's sixty. And at Overlake Christian Church, it's more than a hundred. With so many workers coming and going, it's easy to see how even nursery-specific items can get misplaced.

You think having fewer workers might help, but you need all those workers to care for all those kids. Besides, it's awfully hard to fire volunteers. Before you start nailing down disposable diapers, here are several less drastic steps you can take to rein in your wandering tape player, as well as other less mobile supplies.

Keep larger, more expensive supply items (such as wandering tape players) in your office or a locked supply room. Make them available to teachers on a check-out basis. Encourage teachers to reserve these items early and return them promptly so they'll be available for everyone.

Keep teaching materials in enclosed storage bins. Enclosed bins make it easy to transfer materials between teachers. Better yet, give each teacher his or her own materials—bin and all.

Post a supply list in each nursery room. List basic supplies and their locations in the room and special supplies teachers may request from you. For optimum efficiency, have teachers cross off disposable items (such as diapers and diaper-changing supplies) as they're used up. When you're ready to make a supply run, you can simply check the lists to see what items are needed.

Map out your room. Draw, label, and post a diagram of your room. If you include furniture as well as supply locations, other users of your room will be able to leave things exactly as they found them.

Clearly label shelves and cabinets. If you provide a clearly marked place for everything, volunteers will be more likely to return things to their rightful homes. For volunteers who notoriously ignore posted maps and lists, politely make things obvious by labeling shelves, bins, and cabinets—top and bottom, inside and out.

Formulate a nursery-use policy, and put it in writing. Include requirements for scheduling room use, using nursery equipment, and cleaning up for the next user. If possible, have all users sign a copy of the policy before using the room.

Lock your nursery rooms when they're not in use. Besides ensuring that supplies stay put, you'll be keeping unwanted dirt and germs out of babies' way.

Safe cribs and swings await the soft sighs of peaceful slumber. Clean toys sparkle in readiness for little hands to pick them up. Your nursery's physical environment is complete. Believe it or not, that was the easy part. Now you face the challenging and important task of finding patient, loving workers to care for your nursery attendees.

Section 3:

CRADLE ROLLOVER

Recruiting and keeping quality workers for your nursery

WHAT DO I DO IF...?

Developing written policies for your nursery

"We believe that our children are the Christian leaders of tomorrow. The mission of our preschool department is to encourage all aspects of your child's development: physical, intellectual, social, emotional, and spiritual."

PRESCHOOL POLICIES
FIRST BAPTIST CHURCH
DECATUR, GEORGIA

What is the mission of your church nursery? To provide a safe and caring environment for children? To ensure that children's church times are happy times? To provide a foundation for children's developing faith? You may think your nursery's mission includes all of these things and more. But unless you've formulated and publicized a mission statement, your mission may never implant itself in the hearts and minds of church members, parents, or even workers.

A well-thought-out nursery mission statement is the first step to compiling a complete nursery manual that includes specific ministry objectives, parent guidelines, worker policies, and health and safety procedures. Creating and maintaining a safe and caring nursery takes time, effort, and a lot of prayer. By compiling—and using—a nursery manual, you'll ensure that everyone who comes into contact with your nursery program understands and follows the policies you've worked so hard to develop.

A Manual...for Our Church...Really?

If the idea of written nursery procedures is new or confusing to you, you're not alone. As I talked with nursery workers around the country, only a few churches provided me with a complete set of nursery policies. Others had materials in development, and some had few written policies at all. My own church has a list of nursery policies for workers, but I don't think many parents have seen them. As a result of writing this book, I hope to help change that. These are some of the questions I know I'll be facing. And as you develop and record policies for your nursery, you'll face them too.

Our nursery is so small...do we really need a manual? Yes. It doesn't have to be fancy, and it doesn't have to be lengthy. And if you already have procedures, you don't have to start over. Start by listing procedures (whether written or not) that you already use. Add any additional policies you've developed as a result of reading this book. Type, copy, staple, and distribute.

We'd like to develop a manual, but how will we enforce the policies? People are more likely to follow policies that they've had a hand in developing. When First Baptist Church in Columbia, Tennessee, wanted to revise its nursery handbook, preschool ministries director Tammy Ross created a preschool committee. This ten-member group developed a revised set of policies that were then voted on by the entire church at its annual business meeting. In addition to Tammy, First Baptist's committee included a writer, a lawyer, a public school teacher, someone with medical knowledge, and several preschool Sunday school teachers.

When needed, the committee is available to help enforce the policies. But according to Tammy, reminders are usually the only "enforcement" necessary. Since everyone has read and agreed to the policies, most parents and workers are glad to abide by them.

If we insist on a manual, will workers feel we don't trust them? Maybe at first. But if workers truly have children's best interests at heart, they'll understand when you explain that the manual will help all of you provide the best possible care for the children in your church. If you've already committed yourself to providing a safe and caring nursery, it may help to point out that most of the "new" policies are simply verbally agreed-upon procedures that you've put on paper.

Our workers already know our policies. Why should we put them in writing? Because people are human, and sometimes they forget things. A written manual can include policies that workers aren't likely to use often but may need to know in the event of an accident or emergency.

Although workers may know your policies, parents probably don't—but they'd like to. Parents—especially visitors—who know that well-thought-out procedures govern the nursery will feel much safer leaving their children in your care. And if a dispute about procedures ever does arise (a parent arriving to claim a child without a proper identification tag, for example), the manual can help workers explain the reasons for the policies they find themselves having to enforce.

What Should Our Manual Include?

Your nursery manual should include any and all existing policies or procedures that pertain to your nursery's facilities, equipment, workers, parents, and children. It should also include guidelines for handling legal issues such as accidents or misconduct allegations. The following questions will help you develop or refine nursery policies for each of these areas.

Facilities
- Who may use the rooms?
- How will room use be scheduled?
- Will you require users to leave the rooms as they found them?
- Who will clean the rooms?
- What regular cleaning procedures will be followed?
- Will rooms be locked? Who will have keys?

Equipment
- Who will purchase equipment?
- Will you accept donated equipment? If so, who will inspect it?
- Who will clean and sanitize equipment?
- What regular cleaning procedures will be followed?
- Where will supplies be stored?
- What supplies should be in the nursery at all times?

Legal Issues
- How will you handle cases of suspected child abuse?
- How will you handle accusations of worker misconduct?
- How will you handle natural disasters and weather-related emergencies?

- How will you handle accidents?
- How will you treat children or workers with infectious diseases such as AIDS or HIV?

─────────────── NURSERY NOTE ───────────────

These are only a few of the legal issues that could impact your church nursery. For a comprehensive explanation of these and other issues, check out **The Good Shepherd Program** by William T. Stout and James K. Becker. This easy-to-use program is designed to help churches and church leaders develop procedures and practices that can reduce their risks of abuse and accidental injury. It includes sample policies and forms (hard copy and computer diskette), background checking resources, training outlines, and a host of other resources to help you ensure the safety of your church's children. The Good Shepherd Program is available from Nexus Solutions (1-888-639-8788).

Workers
Potential Workers
- What qualifications must a nursery worker have?
- Will parents work in your nursery?
- Will teenagers work in your nursery?
- Will you have paid nursery workers?
- How many children will you allow per worker?
- Will you do confidential background checks on nursery workers?
- Who will perform the background checks?

Current Workers
- How often and how long will workers serve in the nursery?
- Who will be responsible for finding substitute workers if needed?
- How will you distribute information and materials to workers?
- What health and safety routines must workers know and follow?
- What training opportunities will you provide for your workers?
- Will workers be required to attend training sessions?
- Under what circumstances can a worker be dismissed?

Parents
- What supplies do you expect parents to bring for their children?
- May parents stay with their children in the nursery?
- May parents come to check on their children in the nursery?

- How will parents be located if they are needed?
- How will parents check their children in and out of the nursery?
- How will parents communicate children's special needs, if any?
- How will you communicate with parents about nursery news, needs, or special events?
- How would you like parents to be involved in your nursery ministry?

Children
- What ages of children are included in your nursery program?
- What ages are grouped together in each room?
- Who will decide when a child will be moved to another room?
- Under what circumstances will a sick child be denied admission to the nursery?
- Will snacks be served to children?
- Will children participate in potentially messy activities?

ROCK-A-BYE RECRUITMENT

How to recruit and maintain
volunteer nursery workers

*"I'm scared to leave
my baby with a class full of kids
and just two or three volunteers.
I usually end up going in myself."*

"Doell27"

from America Online

How many nursery workers does it take to establish a safe and caring nursery? According to *Early Childhood Ministry and Your Church* (Kathleen Lull Seaton, et al.), any group of children, no matter how small, should be staffed by at least two adults. Ideally, you should have three workers with every group of children. When three adults are present, one worker is available to leave the room if needed (to find the parent of a crying child, for example) while the other two stay with the children. The presence of more than one worker also safeguards your children (and your church) against potential misconduct allegations or situations.

The larger your nursery, the more workers you'll need. Newborn nurseries should have the lowest worker-to-child ratios. One worker for every three babies is acceptable; one worker for every two babies is even better. (Remember, newborns may need to be held most of the time, and workers only have two arms!) For older infants and toddlers, it's best to provide one worker for every three to four children. For two-year-olds, you can plan on one worker for every four to six children. The following chart will help you determine how many workers you need for your nursery program.

HOW MANY WORKERS DO YOU NEED?

Number of Children	Age of Children		
	Infants	Toddlers	Two-Year-Olds
5	3 workers	3 workers	3 workers
10	3-5 workers	3 workers	3 workers
15	5-7 workers	4-5 workers	3-4 workers
20	7-10 workers	5-7 workers	4-5 workers
25	8-12 workers	6-8 workers	4-6 workers
30	10-15 workers	8-10 workers	5-8 workers
40	14-20 workers	10-14 workers	7-10 workers
50	17-25 workers	13-17 workers	9-13 workers
75	25-37 workers	19-25 workers	13-19 workers
100	34-50 workers	25-34 workers	17-25 workers

Remember that if you have more than fifteen children of any age, you'll need to add additional rooms to prevent overcrowding. (Refer to the "Many Rooms" chart on page 16 for specific children-per-room recommendations.) Also keep in mind that in most churches, attendance is spread over two or more sessions. To figure how many workers you'll need for each session, divide the number of recommended workers by the number of services where nursery care is provided.

Whew! That's a lot of volunteers. Will these worker-to-child ratios really make your nursery that much better? Yes! Heeding the recommended worker-to-child ratios will definitely make your nursery a safer, happier place for everyone.

In addition to providing a safer environment and better care for the babies, keeping low worker-to-child ratios can also benefit your workers and your nursery program. Nursery workers who aren't overwhelmed with too many children will be less tired and more likely to volunteer again. Workers with fewer children to care for are also likely to be more sensitive to each child's needs.

Recruiting Nursery Workers: Where Do I Start?

Babies are innocent, cute, and cuddly. So why aren't church members lining up outside your office to volunteer to work in the nursery? We live in a busy society, and church members have family and work commitments that fill up most of their time. Some are already involved in other church ministries. Others have exhausted their available volunteer hours with school, sports, or community activities. A few may even be intimidated by all those helpless, screaming—oops, I mean cute and cuddly infants.

In one of his cuter, cuddlier moments, Micah clambered into the bathtub with a dry bar of soap. "Soap," he said as he dropped it into the water. "Drop." "Oh!" he exclaimed as he reached for the soap, only to have it slip out of his hands. "Oh! Oh! Oh!" He must have had the soap in his hands a dozen times before he finally lifted it out of the water. Sometimes recruiting is like that. You think you have your nursery fully staffed, but then a worker "slips out of your hands"—a parent doesn't show up to work; a paid caregiver calls in sick; a young married couple is going out of town for a long weekend. So you call and call, and after a dozen tries, you finally manage to "get your hands on" one volunteer.

Recruiting is a time-consuming, often frustrating job, but good workers are an essential part of any safe, caring nursery environment. "About 10 percent of our workers volunteer," said Jennifer Gilbert, a volunteer nursery coordinator in Boulder, Colorado. "The rest are recruited." Yes, recruiting is an inevitable task. But it doesn't have to be a dreadful one. If you're looking for a change from basic bulletin inserts and frenzied phone calling, try one of these five innovative recruitment ideas.

Invite church members to "Come to the Cradle." Have someone in your church take slide photos of the babies in your nursery. Show the slides during services as you play the song "Come to the Cradle" from Michael Card's CD *Come to the Cradle*. This beautiful lullaby reminds parents—and in this case, potential nursery volunteers—that infanthood is a precious, fleeting time and encourages them to set aside their busyness and come catch a glimpse of God's love in the innocent face of a trusting young child. Introduce the slide show with a brief description of your nursery and its need for workers; then show the slides, play the music, and let the images of precious children work on people's hearts.

Encourage adult Sunday school classes to sign up for

"Back to Babyhood" month. At Scottsdale Bible Church in Scottsdale, Arizona, several adult Sunday school classes voluntarily cancel themselves for a month in the summer so class members can serve in the nursery. While most churches don't have enough adult classes to make this a yearlong program, "Back to Babyhood" is a great way to get additional volunteers for those difficult summer months when regular workers may be out of town.

Pass the love along. When Nita Privette's church in Knoxville, Tennessee, needed to generate new enthusiasm (and new workers) for its nursery program, it developed a program called "Passing the Love Along From Generation to Generation." The church asked entire families—including grandparents, if present—to sign up for monthlong terms of service in the nursery. In just a few weeks, twenty-four families had signed up. Volunteers wore buttons that said, "I'm playing in the nursery this month and loving it!" or "I'm a rocking grandpa/grandma" (for grandparents).

NURSERY NOTE

To guard against potential misconduct allegations, it's best to avoid staffing a nursery entirely with workers from a single family. Family members can still work together but should be joined by at least one additional person.

Recruit for the future. At Eugene Christian Fellowship (ECF), where parents are required to serve in the nursery, "recruitment" starts when a new baby is born. Only it doesn't feel like recruitment—to the nursery director or the parent. Here's how it works: The nursery coordinator keeps a list of families who are expecting. When a baby is born, the family receives a card and basket with a gift for Mom, a gift for baby, and information about the church nursery. (Gifts for dads would also be well-received!) Since ECF's nursery serves children four months and older, official recruitment is still several months away. Parents who receive the gift baskets appreciate the church's efforts to welcome their new arrivals. Even a small gift is a much better introduction to the nursery than a "when can you work?" phone call.

Have regular "Nursery News" updates in your Sunday services. At Heritage Church in Moultrie, Georgia, weekly Ministry Moments often feature nursery workers. Volunteers share stories about what's happening in the church's nursery ministry as well as any current needs the ministry might have. A sign-up sheet is available for those interested in participating in the nursery ministry.

To make your "Nursery News" even more compelling, feature "live updates" from babies and toddlers. Have nursery volunteers or other church staff introduce one or two young visitors; then carry babies or lead toddlers around the sanctuary. Church members will enjoy seeing (and probably hearing) babies up close. As the congregation laughs at tales of baby antics, remind them that they can join in the fun by volunteering in the nursery. Make volunteering even easier by providing sign-up sheets on the spot. (Design your own or use the photocopiable "Nursery Interest Inventory" on page 77.)

Whatever you do, don't give up! If one recruitment idea bombs, try another one. Keep trying until you've recruited all the workers you need. Commit yourself to staffing levels that'll make your nursery a safe and caring place—even if it means limiting the number of children you can accept. At Golden Hills Community Church in Brentwood, California, the nursery closes when it gets too full. "When we do get full, which has happened twice in the year that I have volunteered, we put up a sign on the door explaining [that the nursery is too full to accept any more children]," said Suzanne Martin, a parent volunteer at Golden Hills. Parents who arrive after the nursery is full may volunteer to stay in the nursery with their children or may take their children to a "comfort room" where they can view the service on a video monitor.

Turning children away may seem cold or uncaring, but it's better than subjecting them to crowded, unsafe conditions. If you find yourself closing your nursery doors regularly, it's probably time to hit the recruiting trail again. At Golden Hills, full nurseries signal the nursery division leader that more workers are needed to keep up with the church's growth. According to Suzanne Martin, parents at Golden Hills have been very understanding about the policy. "I guess they feel that it is a privilege to have the option of this free child care, so that they may worship the Lord," she said. "The parents also learn to come earlier so that it doesn't happen to them again."

Come One, Come All?

You've carried out your great recruitment ideas, and now you've got more nursery workers than you know what to do with. (OK, so you've got a few new recruits—but it's more than you started with!) Do you pass out burp cloths to everyone who steps forward, or should you be a little more selective?

Although it may seem odd to consider turning away volunteers, it's important to select your nursery workers carefully—even if it means turning some people away. Most volunteers are loving, caring church members who truly desire to serve the Lord by teaching children. But others' motives may not be as pure. Unless your church screens every person to pass through its doors, potential child abusers could enter your midst. However, they're much less likely to enter your nursery if you make a regular policy of screening volunteers. Protect your precious little ones by requiring a written application, interview, and background check of every volunteer, including parents.

Wondering where to start? The Good Shepherd Program recommends that volunteers be active members of a church for at least six months before they may apply for a children's ministry position. Each applicant should also be required to fill out a volunteer ministry application that requests the following information:

- personal identification information;
- a description of previous ministry involvement;
- a description of previous work with babies and children (church and non-church);
- a description of employment history, including explanations for any gaps in employment; and
- the names and phone numbers of at least three references.

The Good Shepherd Program also recommends that applicants sign a declaration that they...

- agree to follow the ministry guidelines carefully;
- do not have a history of abusing children, disciplinary actions or employment problems related to their treatment of children, or a criminal record; and
- give permission and waive liability for reference checks and inquiries into all information provided in their applications or interviews.

The Good Shepherd Program (Nexus Solutions, 1996) provides samples of applications and other volunteer screening forms. Sample volunteer applications and other photocopiable documents can also be found in *No-Work Paperwork for Children's Ministry* (Group Publishing, 1996).

After you've evaluated volunteer applications, you'll want to speak to each potential worker during a face-to-face interview. The interview provides an opportunity for you to get to know the workers in your program, and it offers one more opportunity for you to spot any potential problems. You may also use this time to briefly go over your nursery manual and answer any questions the volunteer might have.

Volunteers whose applications and interviews are satisfactory may move on to the next step: background checks. Background checks conducted through various agencies allow you to find out important information about potential volunteers' criminal histories. According to the federal Child Protection Act of 1993, government agencies are required to assist you in gathering the information you need. Check with your local police department or social services agency to find out how your state handles background checks.

Think twice before you dismiss background checking as a step that only large or inner-city churches need to take. The Good Shepherd Program points out the following consequences of failing to screen, should a negative incident occur in your church:

- You could cause lifelong harm to the victim(s).
- You could ruin your church's ability to witness and spread the gospel.
- You could devastate volunteers' lives and careers—even if allegations are false.

Once you've completed the entire application process, it's time to decide which workers will serve in your nursery. If you're in doubt about whether to accept a volunteer, seek a second opinion if necessary. Your pastor, an experienced nursery worker, or another church staff person may be able to help you complete your evaluation and make a final decision.

Finally, workers you've accepted should receive copies of your manual. After they've read and reviewed it, have them sign an acknowledgment stating they agree to abide by its policies.

You Made It!

Recruiting and maintaining a volunteer staff may seem like a daunting task, but its rewards are eternal in the lives of the little ones you'll serve. So don't be discouraged! Be excited about all the ways your nursery can serve the babies and families in your church. And commit your nursery ministry to the Lord. Ask other church workers to join you in praying that God will prepare the hearts of willing workers and lead them to join you in ministry.

"Let us not become weary in doing good, for at the proper time we will reap a harvest if we do not give up" (Galatians 6:9).

RECRUITMENT EXTRA:
TO PAY OR NOT TO PAY?

Should you have paid workers in your nursery? At Columbia Presbyterian Church in Decatur, Georgia, a paid worker stayed for nearly four years and developed an excellent rapport with the children. Eugene Christian Fellowship (ECF) also employs a paid worker for all its Sunday services. "I don't know what we'd do without her," early childhood coordinator Bonnie Temple said. In addition to providing welcome continuity from week to week, ECF's paid nursery worker also launders crib linens and handles all diaper changes to ensure cleanliness and hygiene.

As I interviewed people in churches, fewer than half paid nursery workers for regular services. I was surprised to discover that Scottsdale Bible Church—a church with over four thousand attendees—has no paid nursery workers. When I asked why, Dawn Martin, Scottsdale Bible's part-time nursery coordinator, explained that the church viewed the nursery as a ministry and wanted to develop a ministry mentality in its workers as well.

Of course it's possible for paid workers to view their jobs as ministries. Pastors and professional Christian educators certainly do. But I was intrigued by the idea of staffing a huge church nursery program entirely with volunteers. How could an all-volunteer nursery staff maintain the continuity that many churches rely on paid workers to provide?

"Some [volunteers] have been doing it for years," Dawn said. Over the years, Scottsdale Bible has steadily recruited workers. By requesting volunteers to give a one-year commitment, they've managed to keep the same friendly faces greeting children week in, week out in at least six of eight birth to two-year-old classrooms.

To pay or not to pay? If you can find a worker who views nursery caregiving as a ministry, the question is worth considering. And paying workers may not cost as much as you think. *The Nurturing Nursery* (Debbie Paschang, et al.) recommends that adult nursery workers be paid slightly more than the current minimum wage. But even if you do use paid workers, you'll probably still need volunteers. "One or two paid workers, even ones who have a lot of experience with children, cannot adequately manage to care for fifteen to twenty children," said Pam Cooper, volunteer nursery coordinator at Heritage Church in Moultrie, Georgia. Although Pam raved about her church's paid workers, she still noted, "Our volunteers are one of our greatest assets."

WHAT GOES AROUND COMES AROUND

Parents as nursery workers

"When we had our son 22 months ago, and would check him into our church's nursery on Sundays, I heard God's words telling me to become a volunteer. After all if somebody was willing to watch my child while I got a dose of God's word, I could very well do the same for them."

SUZANNE MARTIN
ANTIOCH, CALIFORNIA

Parents. They know babies. They love babies. They understand the need for quality care. Who better to staff your church nursery?

Suzanne Martin, a parent at Golden Hills Community Church, loves working in the nursery. "It is so pleasant to see such proud parents each week handing over their little treasures with full confidence that they will be cared for as if they were our own," said Suzanne. "It has been fun to see the children grow and change, wondering what God has in store for them, and if I have been some influence in their new little lives."

Other parents would prefer not to work in the nursery, for a variety of reasons. They're tired. They've had their fill of squalls and wails. They need time for rest and worship. Or they've already committed to serve in other ministries—such as teaching classes for older children, serving communion, or leading in worship. Our pastor and his wife recently had a baby. Since his responsibilities include preaching weekly sermons, of course no one expects him to work in the nursery. But even parents with no responsibilities sometimes want to set aside their "mommy" or "daddy" hats so they can be free to enjoy a refreshing time of worship.

So should you have parent workers or not? Barbara Curtis, veteran parent, said not necessarily. "Caring for the church's children should be the responsibility of the whole church family, not just the families with kids." Barbara Long, veteran nursery worker, says that "the parents should be as responsible for the children as anyone else." Hmm. Both perspectives are valid. Perhaps it's best to let the parents decide.

According to a study by Ellen Galinsky, co-president of the Families and Work Institute in New York City, a warm relationship between caregivers and children is one of the most important factors in establishing a quality child-care environment. Parents (or any nursery workers) who volunteer to work in the nursery because their love for children (including their own) calls them to do so are more likely to develop warm, loving relationships with the babies in the nursery. If parents work in the nursery because they feel guilty or simply because they're required to, the children will notice.

Connie Sylvester, nursery coordinator at Christ Community Church in Charlottesville, Virginia, suggested that parents and other volunteers are more likely to want to get involved if they feel somehow connected to your nursery ministry. After several unsuccessful attempts to get parents and workers to use name tags, Connie had given up trying. But when a parent expressed concern about nursery security and was invited to give input, then a working system was developed. Parents will support a nursery and its policies when they perceive that it's meeting their needs.

By contrast, parents who grudgingly commit to a mandatory nursery-service requirement but remain otherwise uninvolved in your nursery ministry are less likely to take their commitment seriously. "We tried using parents," said Jennifer Gilbert, a volunteer nursery coordinator in Boulder, Colorado, "but they were the biggest no-shows." Jennifer's church chose not to push the issue and now uses only a few parent volunteers. Linda Byram of Overlake Christian Church agreed. "Parent enforcement didn't seem to work in the long run," Linda said. Overlake Christian Church now requires parents to be "on call" only as substitute workers.

Eugene Christian Fellowship (ECF) took a different approach to their problem with no-shows. ECF, which requires parents to work in the nursery once a month, decided to allow parents no more than two no-shows. If parents fail to show up or find a replacement worker a third time, they lose their nursery privileges for a month. According to ECF's early childhood coordinator, Bonnie Temple, the policy seems to be working. "It sounds harsh, but we've never had to enforce it," Bonnie said.

So think twice about requiring parents to work in the nursery. It could create more problems than it solves. Or it could be just the solution you're looking for. Parents may be pleasantly surprised at the ways they can benefit from working in the nursery. "Volunteering periodically is the best way to feel confident about the care," said parent worker Joanne Trahan of Shadow Hills Baptist Church in Las Vegas, Nevada. As you consider using parent volunteers, the following "unexpected rewards" may help parents perceive nursery service as a worthwhile investment of their time. Volunteering...

- allows parents to get to know others in your church.
- allows parents to get to know the nursery staff.
- helps new parents become more comfortable with babies.
- allows parents to become more familiar with (and often more understanding of) the nursery and its policies.
- allows parents to observe firsthand the kind of care their child is receiving.
- allows spouses to minister together.

You may want to consider posting a copy of the "Peekaboo Surprises for Volunteers" handout (p. 76) near your nursery to remind nursery workers of the tangible rewards that come through nursery service.

If you do require parents to work, offer them as many choices as possible. For example, first-time parents who are still learning to care for their own babies may not feel competent to step into a room full of infants. So let them help with cleaning toys or vacuuming rugs. Stay-at-home parents may have had their fill of cries and colic by week's end. But they might be perfectly willing to add your crib linens to their weekly baby laundry. On the other hand, parents who work full time might welcome the chance to spend a few extra hours in the company of precious little ones (including their own). Use the "Nursery Interest Inventory" on page 77 to match potential parent workers with volunteer assignments they'll complete with a smile.

Peekaboo Surprises for Volunteers

Surprise! When you volunteer to work in the nursery you won't just be watching babies. You'll also...

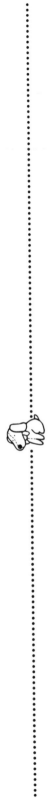

P repare yourself for parenting.

E njoy a ministry with your spouse.

E nable others to worship.

K now the nursery staff.

A cquaint yourself with other families.

B e involved in your child's spiritual development.

O bserve your child's classroom environment.

O pen your heart to the Lord.

NURSERY INTEREST INVENTORY

Dear Nursery Volunteer,

Welcome to our nursery ministry! It's our goal to provide the best possible care and teaching for the little ones in our congregation, and to do that we need your help. We realize that every volunteer is unique, and we want to enable you to serve in an area where you're most comfortable. Please help us make your nursery experience a pleasant one by filling out the interest inventory below.

Your name:

Your address:

Your phone number:

	Gives me pleasure	Doesn't bother me	Makes my stomach turn
INFANT TASKS			
Soothing fussy babies			
Changing diapers			
Talking baby talk			
TODDLER TASKS			
Building towers			
Playing on the floor			
Reading books (again and again)			
Guiding conversation about God, Jesus, and church			
Cleaning up spills			
NURSERY-WIDE TASKS			
Sanitizing toys			
Shopping for supplies			
Laundering crib linens			
Wiping down furniture			
Vacuuming floors			

THE BABY SITTERS CLUB

Selecting and training teenage volunteers

"Teenagers like to do silly things that kids like to do. Sometimes adults feel it's too immature to lower themselves to kids' level and blow bubbles, chase toys, or do what kids like to do."

CHRISTINA SOUTHERN, 17
LAFAYETTE, COLORADO

In addition to being a teenage nursery volunteer, Christina Southern is also our regular baby sitter. We discovered her when we took a parenting class offered by our church. Child care was provided, and Christina was clearly the most competent teenager in the room. We'd been looking for a reliable baby sitter, so we immediately called her up. She loves spending time with Micah—a sentiment he's now beginning to return after hours of bubble blowing, Play-Doh poking, story reading, and other toddler-friendly activities. Without Christina, this book never could have been completed!

When I asked teenage workers what they liked best about working in the nursery, they all responded immediately: "Playing with the kids!" At First Congregational Church in Greeley, Colorado, teenagers work with kids from nursery to third grade. "Young children respond very well to teenagers," said Bob Shaw, church school director at First Congregational. Teresa Millott, a teenage volunteer at Oxnard First Baptist Church in Oxnard, California, agreed. "Older people were kids a long time ago," said Teresa. "Teenagers were kids just a couple years ago. They can remember what kids like to do."

Teenagers may like to play, but do they really know how to take care of babies and young children? I give teenagers a lot of credit, and even I was surprised by the competent answers they gave to my questions about baby and child care. I asked Teresa Millott how she'd handle a crying baby. Right away, she clicked down a list of appropriate responses: Rock the baby, check the baby's diapers, offer the baby a bottle or pacifier, show the baby a new toy. When I asked Christina the same question, she told me about a toddler who used to cry through entire two-hour sessions. After trying activity after activity to stop the tears, she put the little boy in a crib and gently told him that when he stopped crying he could come out and play. The little boy's crying lessened with each session, and after several weeks, had stopped entirely.

You may be pleasantly surprised to discover how much teenagers know about caring for children—especially those with younger siblings or extensive baby-sitting experience. But don't expect them to know everything. And don't expect parents to trust them as much as you do—at least, not at first. According to Bob Shaw, parents prefer to see an adult in charge of the nursery but can grow confident in mature teens over time. Bob has seen this happen at his church, where a responsible high school junior now even manages younger teen nursery workers.

Teenagers have special gifts, but they also have special needs. They like to talk to each other. They like to be with their friends. Sometimes they get distracted—just as adults do! With a little training, encouragement, and respect, you'll see your teenagers rise to, or even surpass, your expectations. The "Terrific Teens" suggestions on page 80, submitted by churches who've used teen workers successfully, will help you provide your teenagers—and your little ones—with the best possible nursery experience.

TERRIFIC TEENS

From Scottsdale Bible Church

- Have teenagers begin as helpers with one or more adults present.
- Have no more than two teenagers working together in any nursery room.
- Start young teenagers with toddlers. Stick with adults or mature high schoolers for infant rooms.
- Communicate these three expectations to teenagers right away:
1. Be on time.
2. Serve the children.
3. Help the lead teacher.

From Eugene Christian Fellowship

- Teenagers who are interested in working in the nursery need to be teachable, helpful, and respectful.
- Teenagers need to be on the floor playing with the kids, not talking to each other.
- Teenagers need to be required to interact with every child at least once to keep them from "playing favorites" with the kids.
- Let parents know what their teenagers are committing to.

From Oxnard First Baptist Church

- Require teenagers to notify their lead teachers when they'll be gone.
- Ask your youth director to recommend mature teenagers who might make good nursery workers.
- Don't let teenagers work in the nursery all the time. They need to be involved in worship and youth activities too.
- Give teenagers a chance. Some may be future teachers; others may discover quickly that nursery work is "not their thing."

All around the country, teenagers are ministering to young children. Will they find a place in your nursery ministry?

FROM CUDDLES TO COLIC

Training tips for
nursery workers

*"I'm always amazed at people's
unwillingness to be trained."*

CATHY
BOULDER, COLORADO

When Cathy scheduled a training for her workers, only three people showed up. "I guess people just think they know how to do it," she said, shrugging her shoulders. After a similar showing, Pam Cooper of Heritage Church in Moultrie, Georgia, has concluded that "people don't respond well to nighttime training sessions."

Training volunteer workers can be a sticky subject. You can decide what topics will be covered. You can come up with creative ways to communicate those topics. You can invite guest speakers, show videos, provide refreshments. You can announce the training with clever posters, skits, or bulletin inserts. But you can't make people come. Or can you?

At First Baptist Church in Columbia, Tennessee, teachers are required to sign a copy of the church's "Preschool Ministries Handbook." The handbook covers workers in nursery through kindergarten classrooms and includes this policy: "All teachers/workers should participate in teacher/worker training sessions that are offered. Teachers/workers are expected to know and follow all policies and guidelines." First Baptist's teachers and workers know when they sign up that participation in training is part of their volunteer commitment. And they're willing to be trained because they know the training they receive will truly meet their needs as they minister to babies and preschoolers.

Once a month, the preschool teachers at First Baptist in Columbia are invited to come to "Partners in Preschool." This innovative program incorporates networking and fellowship with worker training. The topics vary from month to month, and preschool workers from other churches are invited to participate. Ideas are shared, new friendships are formed—and workers come away encouraged.

Workers who feel nurtured and encouraged will want to be trained. Workers who feel used or unappreciated will resist giving even an extra second of their time for training. Before you start any worker training program, check the emotional climate of your volunteers.

● Does each worker feel that his or her abilities are being used to the fullest?

● Does each worker fully embrace your current nursery philosophy and its corresponding policies and procedures?

● Does each worker really know how much you appreciate his or her service?

If you answered "no" to any of these questions, you may need to spend some time preparing the hearts of your workers before a training program will succeed. Not sure where to start? Check out "Diaper Delights"—a collection of great ideas to encourage your workers (pp. 89-90).

When you think you're ready to begin training, the following ideas will help you get off to a successful start:

Respect people's schedules. Offer workers a choice of several times before you put a training meeting on the calendar. Overlake Christian Church discovered that people had a hard time committing to a daylong training event. So they schedule their major annual teacher training as a two-part event. Teachers come Friday evening and then return Saturday morning.

Start small. If you're unsure about scheduling an entire meeting or event, incorporate training into your regular schedule. Have workers arrive fifteen minutes before your scheduled services so you can train them on a single issue or procedure. Take ten minutes to explain the procedure (for example, how to change a diaper), and then allow five minutes for questions. The "Chirps, Burps, and Other Baby Business" handouts make great "minitraining" materials when used individually.

Train as you go. Sometimes the best training is hands-on. Scottsdale Bible Church holds teacher training sessions twice a year. Nursery workers who come on board between sessions are regularly paired with more experienced workers so they can receive "on the job" training. Sharing their experience with others makes workers feel important and helps them refresh themselves on nursery policies and procedures.

Stick to the basics. Volumes have been written on baby and child care. (I can see at least half a dozen books on my shelf from where I'm sitting right now!) Limit your training to topics your volunteers will use. If volunteers want more in-depth information, refer them to one of the child-development resources listed in the "Sources for Nursery Materials" appendix (pp. 141-142).

Take advantage of training opportunities available in your community. Most hospitals offer a variety of child-care classes that could benefit your workers. Nearly all offer CPR or first-aid training. Nancy Rodolph, children's pastor at First United Methodist Church in Clinton, Oklahoma, pays for her two paid nursery attendants to receive CPR training at the local hospital each year. At only fifteen to twenty-five dollars per person, it's a worthwhile investment. Some organizations, such as the American Red Cross, may even be willing to hold a class at your church. If you don't have enough volunteers for a class, invite parents (whether volunteers or not) and other church members to participate. Or get together with another church nursery staff.

Customize your training. Read through the "Chirps, Burps, and Other Baby Business" training topics (pp. 84-88). You can use these ideas as a complete training meeting or pick and choose the ideas that'll work with your volunteers. You may need to add additional activities that relate to specific items in your particular nursery program. In addition to the specific skills training provided by the handouts, include activities that will...

- allow workers to get to know each other,
- orient workers to your nursery facilities,
- familiarize workers with your nursery policies, and
- help workers feel comfortable caring for babies.

May God bless your efforts as you prepare your workers for ministry!

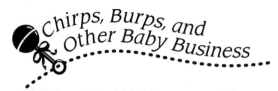

Diaper Changing

- Keep babies and toddlers in full view while changing their diapers.

- Lay the baby or toddler on a washable pad. If the pad is on a changing table, fasten the safety straps.

- Put on a clean pair of disposable gloves and change the baby. Don't use any creams or powders unless parents request and provide them.

- Place the soiled diaper, gloves, and wipes in a disposable bag.

- Drop the bag in a childproof wastebasket lined with a disposable liner.

- Put the baby or toddler down.

- Clean the changing surface with bleach solution or other disinfectant.

- Wash your hands.

Talk to the babies as you change their diapers. Look into babies' eyes with a smile on your face, and they'll know you're happy to be taking care of them.

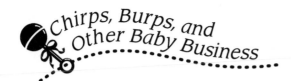

Infant and Toddler Sleep Safety

■ Lay babies (especially those eight months and younger) on their backs or sides. Studies have shown that stomach sleeping may possibly contribute to Sudden Infant Death Syndrome (SIDS). If the baby is old enough to roll over, you may want to prop him or her with a rolled-up blanket.

■ Remove soft bedding or stuffed animals from cribs in which babies are sleeping.

■ Never put a baby down to sleep with a bottle. The sugars in the milk or juice will pool in baby's mouth and cause serious tooth decay.

■ Don't place children over thirty-five inches tall (usually older toddlers) in cribs. They'll probably be more interested in playing than sleeping, and they could possibly climb or fall over the sides. If a toddler is sleepy, fix up a cozy corner with blankets and a pillow.

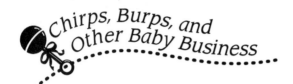

Best Ways to Hold Babies

■ Upright on your lap, face out, so they can see the wonderful world around them.

■ Cradled in your arms so they feel secure.

■ Snuggled against your chest so they can look over your shoulder.

■ Lying on your lap, face down, so you can gently rub or pat their backs.

■ Lying on your outstretched arms so they can see your loving smile.

Best Ways to Calm a Crying Baby

■ Rock the baby gently and slowly in a rhythmic movement.

■ Walk around with the baby.

■ Hold the baby securely over your arm, face down. Rub the baby's back to relieve discomfort caused by gas.

■ Swaddle the baby in a blanket.

■ Sing, read, or talk to the baby in a soft voice.

■ Lay the baby on his or her back. Gently bend the baby's knees to his or her chest.

■ Offer the baby a bottle or pacifier.

Feeding Babies

- Only feed babies the bottles provided by their parents.

- Hold babies in an upright position for feeding.

- Burp babies after feeding. Very young babies may need to be burped halfway through a feeding.

- Hold babies up on your shoulder or face down on your lap for burping. Pat or rub babies' backs until the air in their tummies is released.

- Never warm baby bottles in a microwave, which can heat unevenly.

- Avoid hot plates, which can burn babies (and workers!) if touched.

- Use a baby bottle warmer or Crock-Pot. Fill a baby bottle warmer with water as recommended. Plug it in just before you need to warm a bottle. Fill a Crock-Pot three-quarters full with water, and then plug it in one hour before babies arrive. You can warm bottles with either of these methods in less than a minute.

Feeding Toddlers

- Always inform parents if you'll be serving toddlers a snack.

- Avoid serving drinks in plastic foam cups. Toddlers like to bite them and could choke on the pieces.

- Avoid the following foods, which can cause toddlers to choke:

  - small marshmallows,
  - nuts,
  - sunflower seeds,
  - oranges with seeds,
  - cherries with pits,
  - watermelon with seeds,
  - hard candies,
  - popcorn,
  - raw carrots,
  - raw peas,
  - raw celery,
  - hot dogs,
  - sausage,
  - whole grapes, and
  - caramels

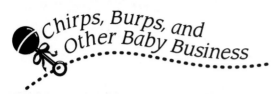

How to Handle Biting

If a child bites another child (first offense)...

- firmly tell the child, "Don't bite. Biting hurts others."

- remove the child from the scene of the conflict. If necessary, isolate the child in a "time out" area for no more than a minute or two.

- discuss the situation with the child in a loving way.

- observe the child to ensure that he or she doesn't bite again.

- Inform the child's parents of the incident. Ask the parent to talk with the child at home.

If you see the child attempting to bite again, interrupt and suggest a better response. For example, you might say, "Did he take your toy? Don't bite. Biting hurts others. Say 'no.' "

If a child bites another child (repeated offenses)...

- immediately call the child's parents.

- have parents help you monitor the child to keep him or her from biting.

If biting continues, ask the parents to remove the child from the nursery.

Explain to the child why he or she is being asked to leave. For example, say, "Nathan, your dad had to leave church to get you because you hurt Michelle. It isn't good to hurt people. We really love you and want you in our class, but you can't come if you continue to hurt people."

DIAPER DELIGHTS

Affirmations and
encouragements for
nursery workers

*"I find working in the church nursery to be
very gratifying. I remember how I looked
forward to getting away from my babies for
a short time and worshiping in church.
Now that my 'babies' are 16 ½ and 18 years
old, working in the nursery helps me re-live
in my mind some of my best memories of
them when they were little."*

MARGARET DEMARCO
WEST SPRINGFIELD, VIRGINIA

Margaret DeMarco has been volunteering in her church
nursery for more than twenty years. She works one
Sunday every other month, year in and year out. She
loves babies and hopes that her nursery work will keep her "current" when she becomes a grandmother one day.

Nursery work can sometimes seem like a thankless job. Volunteers
who love babies find weekly rewards in contented coos, toothless grins,
and toddler hugs. But for every smile, there's also a cry. Every now and
then, nursery workers just need a little boost to keep on cuddling.

To affirm nursery workers for a job well done, Margaret DeMarco
suggested, "It would be nice if the parents who bring their children to
the church nursery would have a little luncheon for the [nursery
workers] once a year, and perhaps present them with corsages which
they could wear to Sunday services on that day."

One flower for a year of serving the Lord by serving the families
in your church—that's hardly too much to ask. Here are other easy

ways for you to let your volunteers know you value their work.

Recognize nursery workers often. When promotion Sunday comes around, many churches take time to recognize Sunday school teachers. But since babies are promoted in and out of various nursery classes all year long, nursery workers often get overlooked. Don't forget to recognize your nursery staff! Even something as simple as listing nursery workers' names in your church bulletin lets them know you value their service.

Create a Nursery Notes newsletter. Include reports from different workers, prayer requests, volunteer schedules, information about upcoming events...the possibilities are endless! At Christ Community Church, a volunteer nursery worker creates the newsletter. She enjoys working on it, and her co-volunteers love reading it.

Meet for "Mugs-n-Muffins." Start a weekly (or monthly) Bible study or fellowship time for teachers. At First Baptist Church, Columbia, Tennessee, teachers meet once a week for a "Mugs-n-Muffins" Bible study. Teachers bring their favorite coffee mug and enjoy an enriching Bible study and prayer. First Baptist's "Mugs-n-Muffins" meets weekday mornings, but you can schedule your fellowship times whenever most teachers are free. Expect modest attendance at first, but as word of the fun and fellowship spreads, more workers may join you.

Have a special volunteer-appreciation dinner. Provide a nice meal at your church or a local restaurant. Invite a motivational speaker or musical performer to address your group. Recap a great year by showing videos or slides of workers and babies. You may even want to invite parents to this event. The more the merrier!

Celebrate your volunteers as you celebrate holidays. Scottsdale Bible Church workers enjoy holiday-themed parties to celebrate their nursery service. One year they held a children's department Christmas breakfast for all the workers, children, and their parents. Another celebration for workers and their families offered a Mexican fiesta theme to coincide with Cinco de Mayo.

Parties and other recognition events are a lot of fun. But don't let them overshadow the simple things. Communicate regularly with your volunteers. Greet workers when they arrive in the nursery. Send thank you notes to substitute workers. Call regular workers at least once a month just to see how things are going. These little things may not seem like much, but together they add up to a happy nursery crew.

Section 4:

ALL ABOUT BABIES

Information and activities to help workers care for babies of all ages

YOU'RE NOT MY MOMMY

Welcoming babies and parents to your nursery

"I've noticed that parents who start leaving their children at a young age (months old) have fewer problems with separation anxiety in the long run. There will always be separation problems at various points, but starting early seems to bring the sense of familiarity earlier."

JOHN BREDESEN
ST. PAUL, MINNESOTA

Like most concerned nursery parents, John Bredesen of Fairmount Avenue United Methodist Church in St. Paul, Minnesota, has "about 4,200 other opinions (give or take a few) about church nurseries." His four-year-old is a near-nursery graduate, and his two-year-old visits the church nursery regularly. As I talked with John Bredesen and other parents about their church nursery experience, many offered advice for dealing with the unavoidable separation anxiety that creeps up when babies are left in another person's care.

"I think first impressions are everything," said Kathy Beckner of West Palm Beach, Florida. "I feel secure leaving my child when I see a warm greeting from the worker and interaction with my child as I am checking her in. If they check her in like she is a piece of luggage, the red flag goes up and I would rather have her in the service with me."

Of course, no child should ever be treated like luggage! But concerned parents can be comforted by the fact that separation anxiety is a natural childhood emotion. Its existence (and persistence!) indicates a strong, healthy attachment between parent and child. Babies know they're loved by Mommy and Daddy, but they're not so sure what kind of care they'll get from these strangers in the nursery. Separation anxiety can begin during the second half of babies' first year and usually peaks around twelve to sixteen months. At eighteen months, Micah still occasionally cries at being put in the nursery, but usually only briefly.

Although it's no fun for babies, separation anxiety may be hardest on parents. They've resolved to put their baby in the nursery, but deep down they're still a tiny bit concerned about leaving their precious child with nursery workers who are barely even acquaintances. Then baby starts to cry, as if there really were something in that nursery to be afraid of. Hmm, the parents think. Maybe this nursery plan wasn't such a good idea. We'll just keep baby with us a little longer. This cycle can continue indefinitely and can prevent parents (and babies) from fully participating in worship and other church activities.

So how can nursery workers best help babies make the transition from Mommy's or Daddy's arms to nursery care? Start by respecting both the parents' and the child's feelings. Acknowledge that sometimes it's hard to leave Mom and Dad. Work with the parents to reassure the child that Mommy and Daddy will be back in a little while. If you're currently experiencing a high level of separation anxiety in your nursery, you may want to offer parents and workers one or more of the following suggestions to help ease the transition.

Make friends. Have parents leave their babies in the nursery as soon as they're comfortable and as regularly as possible. You won't eliminate all traces of separation anxiety, but babies are less likely to fuss at the sight of familiar faces they've seen week after week. In John Bredesen's experience, kids who start attending the nursery earlier "get over [separation anxiety] faster (usually less than a minute or two) because they are familiar with the place, the adults, and with the other kids." When you consider your staffing needs, remember that children will warm up to workers more quickly if they see at least one familiar face each week.

Don't hurry. Allow plenty of time for the parents and child to greet nursery workers and look around the nursery. Make eye contact and talk to each child as you welcome him or her to your nursery.

Help parents point out activities the child has enjoyed in the past. Instead of taking the child from the parent, wait for the parent to hand you the child.

Welcome newcomers. Extend a special welcome to new parents and families visiting your church for the first time. Invite them to look around your nursery facilities, and make sure nursery workers introduce themselves by name. Thank them for trusting their child to your care, and give them a copy of the "Welcome to Our Nursery!" handout (p. 97) and a copy of your church's nursery procedures. Follow up by telling them what activities their child enjoyed in the nursery that day.

Use a sign-in system. Have parents record their child's name, names of persons authorized to pick up their child, and any special needs of the child on a sign-in sheet. (Create your own or use the "Nursery Check-In" handout on page 98.) It may seem like extra paperwork, but parents who use it will be relieved to know that you know their child's name and that you won't release their child to a stranger.

For added security in this area, use a number system. Note the child's number on the sign-in sheet; then give parents a copy of the number to take with them. When they give you the number, you give them their child. If you have a lot of children who attend regularly, you may want to assign them permanent numbers.

Encourage questions. Ask parents to tell you about any special needs their baby may have. Confirm that baby's diaper bag contains clean diapers, clothing, and any special snacks or drinks the baby might need. If the diaper bag doesn't have a tag, label it with the child's name—even if you have to write it on a piece of masking tape. By labeling the bag, you let parents know that you'll make sure the supplies they've packed will be available for their child.

If parents don't have labels for their diaper bags, encourage them to fill out a diaper-bag tag from the handout on page 98. Keep scissors and colorful yarn on hand (out of children's reach, of course!), and you'll have instant identification tags.

Encourage goodbyes. Even though it may cause tears, it's generally best for children to say goodbye and see their parents

NURSERY NOTE

Diaper-bag identification tags make great gifts for new parents. New parents will be surprised and grateful to receive diaper-bag tags the first time they visit your nursery. Just photocopy the handout on page 98, cut out the tags, and fill in the information. For a nicer gift, go to a copy or print shop and have the tags laminated, or "laminate" with clear Con-Tact paper.

leave. Having parents sneak out while a child is distracted can erode the child's trust in his or her parents and in your nursery workers. When babies cry and scream and cling to parents' clothing, sometimes it's best for parents just to leave. Once parents have gone, most children eventually forget their fears and spend the remainder of the class time happily playing, singing, snacking, or doing whatever activities you've provided.

If your nursery has a window or split door that allows babies to see out, ask parents to use discretion when checking on their children during the service. Point out that seeing a parent will likely renew the separation anxiety. Request that nervous parents send a friend to peek in.

Suggest alternate drop-off plans. If a child seems particularly anxious about leaving one parent, Sue Huffman, a nursery parent in Lowell, Michigan, suggests having the other parent or a family friend drop the baby off next time. If someone other than a parent drops off a child, make sure your workers know in advance who'll pick up the child.

Invite parents to join you. If a child (or parent) seems to be having a particularly difficult time, have parents stay and play with their child for a few minutes. Say to the child, "Your mommy (or daddy) is going to stay with us for five minutes and then go to the grown-up class." As parents play with their children, have them continue to provide reassurances such as "Isn't this fun! I'm so glad you get to stay and play here when I go to my class in a few minutes."

A few parents may want stay the whole time. In this case, it's likely that the parent is as anxious about leaving the child as the child is about leaving the parent. It's fine for parents to stay once or twice, and staying may help them feel more confident about the care their baby is receiving. But unless they want to become regular nursery volunteers, kindly encourage them to return to their own activities after two or three sessions.

Provide comfort items. If a child has a special blanket or pillow, encourage parents to bring that item to church. (Don't encourage parents to bring special toys, which can cause problems when other children see and want to play with them.) Esther Stockwell, a nursery worker in Anaheim, California, requests that parents provide the nursery with a picture of themselves and a cassette tape of their voices. When children cry for their parents, she takes them to the picture wall to see and hear a calming reminder that Mommy and Daddy are close by.

Prepare for parents' return. Tell the child, in terms that he or she will understand, exactly when a parent will return. For example, you might say, "Mommy and Daddy will be back after we sing our pick-up song" or "When we come in from the playground, Mommy and Daddy will be here to get you." Plan your class schedule so that the activity you mention is truly the last thing you do with children before parents arrive.

To ease anxious parents' minds, it's also a good idea to have each child's diaper changed shortly before the end of your nursery session. Parents who retrieve a child with a wet (or soiled!) diaper may question the attentiveness of your nursery workers and choose not to return.

Welcome to Our Nursery!

We're glad to provide friendly, loving workers to care for your baby. When you bring your baby to the nursery, you can help our workers by...

- sharing any special needs or concerns you or your child might have.

- providing a labeled diaper bag with extra disposable diapers; fresh clothes; and any bottles, drinks, or snacks your baby will need.

- bringing your child to church in a dry, clean diaper.

- signing in your child and assisting with his or her transition into the nursery as requested.

If your child cries when you drop him or her off, please don't panic! Our workers will work with you to find the best way to comfort your child so you and your baby can enjoy your time at church.

nursery Check-In

Child's name:

....

Parent's name(s):

....

Parent's location:

....

Special needs:

....

....

If you're visiting our church today, please give us your
address and phone number:

....

....

DIAPER BAG
Identification Tag

Child's name:

Parent's name(s):

IF LOST, PLEASE RETURN TO...

Address:

Phone:

WORKS OF WONDER

The amazing, high-speed world of baby development

"Woof, woof."

MICAH WILGER

LAFAYETTE, COLORADO

"**W**oof, woof" were Micah's first words. I think. At least, that's what I wrote in his baby book. But it's hard to remember for sure because since then, his vocabulary has grown exponentially. It now includes words like "outside," "mailbox," and "envelope." I've stopped writing them down because I just can't keep up.

Although language development is Micah's latest developmental milestone, it's not the only one that has sped by. Each time we go to visit Grandma, who lives several hundred miles away, she says, "He's changed so much. I can't believe we thought he was interesting the last time he was here." But of course, we did. Before the talking onslaught, learning to walk was the big thing. Before that, it was crawling. Before that, rolling over. Even when Micah could do nothing more than lie in his crib and cry, we marveled at his very existence.

Babies do change quickly. Right now I'm pretty well-versed in the toddler tango (chasing Micah around the house until I can catch and hug him), but when friends with newborns ask for advice, I have to scratch my head and think a while. The workers in your nursery are there because they love babies—and they all may have a particular stage of babyhood they love best. Some workers—especially teenagers—enjoy older babies and toddlers who are really beginning to communicate. Some nursery volunteers thrill to rock and cuddle newborns. Others consider creepers and crawlers their "specialty." Use the "Works of Wonder" growth charts (pp. 100-105) to remind workers of all the wonderful things babies learn to do as they grow. (For a detailed discussion of babies' spiritual development, see "Kingdom Kids," beginning on page 114.)

Newborn → Three Months

Physical	Baby turns head from side to side.	Baby begins to push self up off the floor.	Baby begins to swipe at objects.	Baby begins to bring both hands together.	Baby rolls in one direction.
Communication	Baby responds to high-pitched voices.	Baby listens when someone is speaking.	Baby looks when someone is speaking.	Baby communicates needs by crying.	
Social/Emotional	Baby coos.	Baby begins to smile at people and toys.	Baby enjoys viewing things from a variety of perspectives.	Baby likes to see self.	Baby likes to listen to sounds, including voices.
Spiritual	Baby learns to trust caring adults.	Baby learns that his or her needs will be attended to.			

Three Months → Six Months

Physical	Baby brings both hands together.	Baby swipes at objects.	Baby rolls in one direction.	Baby begins to grasp objects.	Baby sits unsupported.	Baby bangs two objects together.	Baby begins to creep.
Communication	Baby exchanges coos with familiar caregivers.		Baby responds to his or her name.	Baby babbles "baby talk."	Baby squeals with delight.	Baby recognizes "Mama," "Dada."
Social/Emotional	Baby laughs and giggles.	Baby follows moving objects with his or her eyes.		Baby likes to do things with caregivers.		
Spiritual	Baby responds to happy times at church.	Baby continues to build trust in caregivers.				

Six Months → Nine Months

Physical	Baby swipes at objects.	Baby rolls in one direction.	Baby begins to grasp objects.	Baby sits unsupported.	Baby bangs two objects together.	Baby begins to creep.	Baby pulls self to stand.	Baby uses index finger to point.	Baby walks unsupported.
Communication	Baby begins to understand the meaning of words.	Baby imitates adult sounds.	Baby enjoys communicating with sounds.	Baby begins to understand (but not always obey) "no."	Baby begins to speak consonant sounds.				
Social/Emotional	Baby plays with a single toy repeatedly.	Baby reaches for toys that interest him or her.	Baby may cry when parents leave.						
Spiritual	Baby continues to build trust in caregivers.	Baby begins to associate God and Jesus with good feelings at church.							

Nine Months → Twelve Months

Physical	Baby sits unsupported.	Baby bangs two objects together.	Baby begins to creep.	Baby pulls self to stand.	Baby uses index finger to point.	Baby walks unsupported.	Baby builds a tower.	Baby begins to enjoy scribbling.
Communication	Baby points to things.	Baby turns when his or her name is used.	Baby may say one or two recognizable words.	Baby begins to mimic the sounds of adult speech.	Baby responds to simple instructions.			
Social/Emotional	Baby begins to understand cause and effect (if I bang that drum, it makes a noise).	Baby may cry when parents leave.	Baby enjoys looking at familiar pictures.	Baby may show preference for a favorite toy.				
Spiritual	Baby continues to develop trust in caregivers.	Baby likes familiar nursery workers.	Baby may try to say "Jesus" or other words he or she has heard repeatedly at church.					

Twelve Months → Eighteen Months

Physical	Baby bangs two objects together.	Baby begins to creep.	Baby pulls self to stand.	Baby uses index finger to point.	Baby walks unsupported.	Baby builds a tower.	Baby begins to enjoy scribbling.	Baby enjoys climbing.
Communication	Baby uses single words to stand for thoughts: "down" for "I want to get down."	Baby understands many words and phrases.	Baby listens for a few minutes to stories.	Baby can recognize body parts.	Baby can identify pictures of familiar objects.	Baby begins to replace gestures with words.		
Social/Emotional	Baby begins to pretend.	Baby enjoys playing near, but not with, other babies.	Baby enjoys hearing favorite stories again and again.	Baby may call regular workers by name.				
Spiritual	Baby continues to develop trust in caregivers.	Baby may recognize "God," "Jesus," and "church."	Baby may enjoy going to church.					

Eighteen Months → Twenty-Four Months

Physical	Baby walks unsupported.	Baby builds a tower.	Baby begins to enjoy scribbling.	Baby enjoys climbing.	Baby jumps with both feet.	Baby throws ball overhand.	Baby strings beads.
Communication	Baby begins forming two-word combinations such as "pick up" or "put in."	Baby begins using more verbs.	Baby adds several new vocabulary words each day.	Baby may laugh at words that sound funny or are exaggerated.			
Social/Emotional	Baby understands "mine."	Baby has a hard time sharing.	Baby wants to do things himself or herself.	Baby may throw tantrums.	Baby is easily frustrated.		
Spiritual	Baby continues to develop trust in caregivers.	Baby may recognize "God," "Jesus," and "church."	Baby may enjoy going to church.	Baby may recognize the Bible.	Baby enjoys simple Bible stories and songs.		

Permission to photocopy this handout granted for local church use. Copyright © Jennifer Root Wilger. Published in *The Safe and Caring Church Nursery* by Group Publishing, Inc., P.O. Box 481, Loveland, CO 80539.

GOO-GOO GRINS

Games and activities to light up little faces

"He thinks that's a game?"

TOM WILGER

LAFAYETTE, COLORADO

Micah's latest "game" goes like this: Mom (or another willing adult) sits on the couch, shoes off, feet resting on the coffee table. Micah then proceeds to climb up, on, and over the "bridge" created by the adult's outstretched legs. The game is called Climb, and Micah made it up himself. He requests it nearly every day and is perfectly happy to keep climbing, over and over, for twenty minutes or longer. He thinks it's hilarious fun, especially when he gets enough momentum to push himself over into a primitive somersault. When I explained this "game" to Tom, he laughed and shook his head in disbelief. "Micah, you're a silly boy," he said as he sat down to take his turn.

Although playing games may seem like frivolous activity to adults, to children it's serious business. Dr. Benjamin Spock, author of the classic parenting resource *Baby & Child Care*, said that every time children play make-believe or build with blocks, they're increasing their learning skills. In his article "The Power of Play," Spock said, "It's important to understand and appreciate the value of children's play. Through these often solitary games, young children teach themselves an impressive array of skills" (Parenting, September 1996).

So should you really spend part of your precious hour with these children playing games? Absolutely. Sometimes games will incorporate Christian concepts. Babies love playing Peekaboo and finding someone Jesus loves; hearing you count their fingers and toes, which God made; or looking into a mirror at a smiling face and discovering that church is a happy place. But other games are just for playing. And for babies, playing means learning. All the time.

As churches work hand in hand with parents to foster young

children's growth and development, nursery workers can use games to help babies discover arms that wave, legs that kick, and toes that wiggle. Together, workers and babies can explore toys and objects that shake, rattle, spin, and roll. They can put things in and take things out. They can squeeze, push, pull, pretend. For babies, every interaction is a grand opportunity to assimilate new information.

Playing games with babies can also help your nursery workers learn about individual babies' temperaments. Some babies enjoy lots of motion. They love to laugh and squirm and kick their legs. Other babies prefer quiet games where they can cuddle and coo as they sit securely in a caregiver's lap. Parents know their babies' temperaments, and they'll be thrilled if your workers do too. Just imagine the surprised smile on a mother's face when she hands her child to a nursery worker and hears the worker say, "Welcome, Susie. Let's play Peekaboo. I know that's one of your favorites."

Playing with young children is easy. Anyone can do it. Even grown-ups. By day my husband, Tom, is a sophisticated analyst with advanced degrees in mathematics. But when he comes home from the office and starts playing with Micah, I have to look twice to make sure I don't have two little kids running around the house. Playing games with babies and toddlers will be fun for children and workers if you remember the "P's of Play."

Participate without pressuring. It's OK to initiate a game, but let children help you play it in ways that are fun for them—even if it turns out differently from what you intended.

Provide toys that encourage imaginative play, especially for older babies and toddlers. In addition to purchased toys, playing with oatmeal boxes, plastic margarine tubs, laundry detergent scoops, or empty egg cartons can be great fun for little ones.

Put on the brakes when it's time to stop. When a baby or toddler is tired of an activity, he or she will let you know. Don't insist on continuing a game that's been played out. (Reserve that right for your young playmate, who may want to continue playing long after you're ready to try something else!)

The "Play 'n' Learn" activity handouts (pp. 108-113) invite your workers to set foot in the world of play. Some activities are old favorites; others are brand new. Many incorporate lyrics sung to familiar tunes. All are meant to inspire your creativity as you help little ones discover the wonders of God's world through play.

PLAY 'N' LEARN GAMES
for Newborn to 3 Months

Games for the youngest children should be gentle, quiet activities that encourage babies to exercise their developing bodies. Although babies may not seem to respond much, they enjoy studying caregivers' faces as they come up close for playtime. As babies approach three months of age, they'll probably begin to smile while they play.

So Big

Lay baby down on a blanket or play mat. Hold baby's hands on his or her chest as you ask, "How big is (baby's name)?" Then open baby's arms wide as you say, "(Baby's name) is soo big!" As you repeat the game, add the following variations or make up your own.

How much does God love (baby's name)?

God loves (baby's name) soo much!

How much does (caregiver's name) love (baby's name)?

(Caregiver's name) loves (baby's name) soo much!

Time to Change a Diaper

Even diaper-changing times can be play-times for babies. Sing this song to baby as you change his or her diaper. Nod your head and look baby in the eye as you sing. Sing it to the tune of "Did You Ever See a Lassie?"

Oh, it's time to change your diaper,
Your diaper, your diaper.
Oh, it's time to change your diaper
To get fresh and dry.

Rolling Ribbits

Lay baby on his or her back. Show baby a stuffed frog and say, "Ribbit, ribbit." Jump the frog up and down on baby's tummy a few times. Then move the frog about a foot away from baby. Jump the frog toward baby as you say, "Ribbit, ribbit, ribbit, roll!" When you've jumped the frog right next to baby, use the frog to gently nudge the baby to roll over. Babies will also enjoy stuffed cows (moo, moo, move); rabbits (hop, hop, hop on over); or other animal variations. Tell baby that God made the animals.

Permission to photocopy this handout granted for local church use. Copyright © Jennifer Root Wilger. Published in *The Safe and Caring Church Nursery* by Group Publishing, Inc., P.O. Box 481, Loveland, CO 80539.

PLAY 'N' LEARN GAMES
for 3 to 6 Months

Three- to six-month-old babies can take a more active role in the games you play. They love imitating sounds and gestures made by caregivers. They can reach and grasp at toys, toes, or grown-up fingers. You may be surprised to discover babies helping you create variations as you repeat these games again and again.

Ten Little Toesies

Babies love to play with fingers and toes. Gently grasp each of baby's toes as you sing this song to the tune of "Ten Little Indians."

One little, two little, three little toesies,

Four little, five little, six little toesies,

Seven little, eight little, nine little toesies,

Ten little toes God made.

We Hear These Sounds

Babies love to hear grown-ups make funny sounds. Each time you say, "We hear these sounds," gently grasp baby's ears. You can also help babies wave their arms as you say, "Up and down and all around."

A cow says "moo." A duck says "quack."

A little boy says, "Look at that!"

Up and down and all around,

On the farm we hear these sounds.

A dog says "woof"; a cat, "meow."

A little girl says, "Listen now!"

Up and down and all around,

On our street we hear these sounds.

The wind says "whoosh." The birds say "tweet."

A mommy says, "Night-night, my sweet."

Up and down and all around,

At our house we hear these sounds.

The people sing. The babies coo.

A teacher says, "(Baby's name), God loves you."

Up and down and all around,

At our church we hear these sounds.

Bouncy, Bouncy

Hold baby on your lap and gently bounce him or her up and down as you sing this song to the tune of "Frère Jacques." When you sing, "Stand up tall," help baby to "stand" on your lap—or lift baby up over your head.

Bouncy, bouncy.

Up and down.

Baby (baby's name)'s bouncing.

Up and down.

Bouncy, bouncy.

Look around.

See the things that God made.

All around.

Bouncy, bouncy.

Stand up tall.

Baby (baby's name)'s growing.

Big and tall.

PLAY 'N' LEARN GAMES

for 6 to 9 Months

Six- to nine-month-old babies are on the move. They enjoy games with bigger motions, lots of repetition, and even a few surprises. Peekaboo and patty-cake are great favorites of this age group. Most babies this age can sit well and will enjoy sitting on their own as they join you for playtime.

Is It You?

Babies enjoy finding familiar faces under funny costumes. Cover your eyes, head, or entire face with one of the following props, and let baby find you. Then try putting the hats on baby. Add a mirror for even more fun. Use…

- old sunglasses;
- a baseball cap or other hat;
- a sun visor;
- a clean, empty, plastic flower pot;
- a paper plate; or
- a lightweight box.

I'll Fly Away

Sing songs about heaven, such as "I'll Fly Away" or "Swing Low, Sweet Chariot" as you lift babies over your head and "fly" them around the room.

Roll, Roll, Roll

Put baby on his or her tummy on top of an inflated beach ball. Hold baby tightly as you roll him or her around on the ball. Sing this song to the tune of "Row, Row, Row Your Boat" as you roll baby around. After a few rolls, change the second line of the song to "roll the ball around," and show baby how to roll the ball back and forth. Crawling babies will also enjoy beach ball games such as "Push, push, push the ball. Push it all around."

Roll, roll, roll the ball.
Roll the baby round.
God loves (baby's name); God loves me.
God keeps us safe and sound.

PLAY 'N' LEARN GAMES

for 9 to 12 months

Nine- to twelve-month-old babies are often referred to as pretoddlers, and for good reason. They love to crawl into spaces and discover new things. They can now pick up even small objects (such as cereal loops) and delight in filling-and-dumping games. These older babies are truly becoming social beings and can understand and respond to simple instructions.

Find the Bear God Made

Gather a variety of age-appropriate animal toys. These could be stuffed animals, rattles, teethers, squeakers, or bath toys. Show baby each toy and say, "God made (name of animal)." Then have baby watch as you hide the toy under a blanket. Ask baby, "Can you find the (name of animal) God made?"

Crawl on Through

Cut off two opposite ends of a large cardboard box to create a tunnel for babies to explore. Set baby down on one side of the tunnel; then peek through the other side as you say this rhyme. Once babies catch on to this game, they'll speed through the tunnel before you even finish the first verse!

Baby, baby, crawl on through.
Baby, baby, I see you!

Baby, baby, come on in.
Crawl right in and get your friend!

Baby, baby, on your knees.
God loves you, and God loves me!

Drop It In

Show babies how to drop small objects into a box, plastic jar, or bucket. You can use clothespins, small plastic blocks, or juice can lids. Let babies try dropping a few objects as you repeat the following lines.

Open fingers, drop it in.
Then pick it up and drop again.

Let babies enjoy dropping the objects into the box and then dumping them out. They may also want to bang, stack, or carry the objects. Enjoy their antics as they discover all the ways they can play the game.

PLAY 'N' LEARN GAMES

for 12 to 18 Months

These little ones can walk, climb, and even run. Although they may not play together, they enjoy being in the company of other children. They know what they want—and what they don't want—and they're not afraid to tell you. If they can. Young toddlers usually know more than they're able to communicate, so you may have to make a few guesses before you get their meaning. Communication can be a game in itself when your guesses turn into nonsense words that sound funny!

Church Bus Rides

Let toddlers take turns sitting on a blanket or large towel as you pull them around the room in the "church bus." As they "travel," sing this song to the tune of "Mary Had a Little Lamb."

(Baby's name) likes to go to church,
Go to church, go to church.
(Baby's name) likes to go to church
And ride the big church bus.

Sticky Sticker Stuff

Toddlers love stickers of any kind. Animal stickers can be fun, but even price tags or file-folder labels will do. (It's the sticky part that counts!)

Have toddlers help create new toys by applying stickers to shoe boxes, margarine tubs, or empty two-liter plastic bottles. If you do use picture stickers, name each picture as toddlers attach the stickers. When toddlers finish decorating the items, show them how to roll the bottles, push the shoe boxes, or fill the margarine tubs with small toys.

Bubbles of Love

Toddlers are fascinated with soap bubbles. Each time you dip your bubble stick in bubble solution, say, "God loves (name of baby)." Then shower each child with "bubbles of love." Say, "Look at all the bubbles! God loves (name of baby) lots and lots!"

Older toddlers have recognizable (if not exactly perfect) words for most familiar objects and people. They may even be able to say words like "church," "class," "Jesus," and "God." If they're busy solving a problem (such as removing all the blocks from the shelf), they might not even know you're there, but most of the time they're interested in following you around and doing what you do.

Colors of Love

Cut out colored construction paper hearts, and put them inside clear plastic jars (older toddlers love to unscrew lids) or containers. Let toddlers open the jars and remove the hearts. As they remove the hearts, teach them the following rhyme:

Red heart, red heart, can you guess?
Does God love (name of child)? Yes! Oh, yes!

Repeat the rhyme for each color of heart you've prepared. Be prepared with extra hearts since toddlers are likely to crumple, tear, or otherwise mangle the paper creations. Toddlers also enjoy carrying around pairs of things, so you may want to start out with two hearts in each container.

Puppet Pop Praise

You can make a simple people-powered jack-in-the-box with an old sock, a permanent marker, scissors, and a shoe box.

Use the permanent marker to draw puppet features on the sock. If you have felt or other fabric scraps on hand, you may want to add hair. Be sure all features are tightly attached. Cut a hole in the bottom of the box that's large enough for your hand.

Put the puppet on your hand and put your hand through the hole in the box. Put the lid on the box so the puppet is hidden. Then sing this song to the tune of "Pop! Goes the Weasel":

We thank you, Jesus, for each boy.
We thank you for each girl.
For families, for friends at church,
Pop! Thank you, Jesus.

When you sing "pop!" raise up your hand and knock the lid off the box.

Animal ABCs

Collect pictures of animals starting with each letter of the alphabet. (If you get stuck on some of the more difficult letters, try xanthops, a bird; narwhal, a whale; or urchin, a hedgehog.) Tape the pictures to a wall at toddlers' eye level. Walk around the room and show toddlers the pictures. As you look at each picture, say, "God made (name of animal). (Name of animal) starts with (letter of the alphabet)." When toddlers begin to know the animals (probably after six or eight repetitions), you can simply say, "God made…" and let toddlers fill in the name of the animal you're looking at.

Most of the time, you won't get to all the animals, but toddlers will enjoy seeing them all around the room. And different toddlers will like different animals. From time to time, thank God for all your animal friends.

KINGDOM KIDS

Teaching babies and toddlers about God

"I really have a problem with the term 'nursery.' I take my children to church to learn about God, the Bible, worship, etc. and I want that to start when they're babies. I want every experience my children have at church to be a learning experience, even if that means a baby is learning that church is a good place to be because people here love me."

LORI
FLORIDA

Can tiny children really learn about God? No one would dispute the fact that preschoolers can learn Bible lessons. And most curriculum companies develop—and churches use—teaching materials for two-year-olds. Some have been so bold as to create and implement materials for toddlers. But babies? Infants? Really?

"If Jesus were here, he would do more than just rock them," says Sheila Halasz, a longtime children's program coordinator from Crystal Lake, Illinois. Shelia's church, St. Paul's United Church of Christ, offers children's Sunday school for babies as young as six months old. Teachers lead babies in simple Bible songs and tactile activities. And the babies learn—in their baby ways.

"We started this program when my daughter was thirteen months old," said Shelia, "and I distinctly remember her kicking her car seat excitedly whenever we drove past the church building." Sheila Halasz's daughter is twelve now, but she still remembers some of the puppets she played with in the nursery—and the Bible lessons she learned from them.

According to V. Gilbert Beers, author of *The Toddlers Bible*, it's never too early to introduce the Bible. "Obviously an infant can't memorize Bible verses or learn doctrines," said Beers in his book *Teaching Toddlers the Bible*. "But twos and threes will amaze you with their ability to soak up Bible stories, Bible people, Bible truths. Even an infant will form vibes, growing-up vibes, of a parent, or parents, reading the Bible."

Little children are voracious learners. Even in the womb, babies can sense light and darkness, hear sounds, and react to their mothers' emotions. Long before they can talk, they touch, poke, shake, bang, and even taste things in an effort to discover how the world works. Babies' lives are filled with unspoken questions: What is this thing? Where did it come from? How does it work? As adults, they look to us for answers. Parents and teachers have the privilege of helping babies know the One who created the big, bright world they're so eager to explore.

An infant waves her arms and wonders, What are these? A loving mother gently answers, "You're waving your arms, sweet baby. God gave you arms for hugging, hands for holding, and fingers for touching." Of course the baby doesn't yet know who God is. But as these interactions continue, babies begin to associate the name "God" with the loving, caring parents and teachers who speak it.

Infants develop their earliest feelings about God through experiences with loving, trusted, and seemingly all-knowing caregivers. When their cries are answered and their needs are attended to, these little ones begin to trust. This same trust, nurtured by years of faithful teaching, love, and care, will someday lead them to trust Jesus and choose to love and follow him.

Jesus said, "Therefore, whoever humbles himself like this child is the greatest in the kingdom of heaven. And whoever welcomes a little child like this in my name welcomes me" (Matthew 18:4-5). From an adult perspective, I can't think of a more humbling experience than infancy. Newborn babies are almost completely helpless. Their entire lives are out of their control. They can't feed themselves. They can't see very well. They can't talk. They can only cry and trust that someone will hear and answer.

Infants have a lot to learn about love and trust. But they also have a lot to teach us. Like little children, we cry out to the Lord, "Hear my prayer, O Lord, listen to my cry for help; be not deaf to my weeping" (Psalm 39:12a). And like a loving parent, God answers and takes care of our needs: "I waited patiently for the Lord; he turned to me and heard my cry...he set my feet on a rock and gave me a firm place to stand" (Psalm 40:1-2).

Just as infants trust their parents and caregivers, God wants us to trust him. And when we do, God will give us the wisdom and insight, patience and goodness, faithfulness and love, that we need to teach the precious little ones he's entrusted to our care.

What Can Babies and Toddlers Learn About God?

More than we might think! Infants as young as four to six months old respond to happy times at church. By nine months, infants who have received loving care from parents and caregivers who talk to them regularly about God may begin to associate God and Jesus with good feelings. Early in their second year (thirteen to fifteen months), these babies may even recognize the names of God and Jesus. We bought Micah his first Bible when he was around fourteen months, and it wasn't long before he could name all the characters in it. He can now recognize pictures of Noah, Moses, David, Daniel, and—most importantly—Jesus. As his second birthday draws near and his vocabulary and conversation skills continue to grow, we look forward to reading and talking about more Bible stories together.

When teaching babies, it's best to stick to simple Bible thoughts rather than trying to teach an entire story. Since babies only gradually develop an awareness and acceptance of others, lesson themes should connect closely to babies' experiences. Instead of teaching babies "Jesus loves children," for example, you might use the simpler words "Jesus loves me." The chart on page 117 suggests appropriate Bible thoughts for babies and young toddlers.

Older toddlers and twos can add a few more concepts. In *Teaching Toddlers the Bible*, V. Gilbert Beers suggested these additional topics for toddlers:

- God gives us food.
- God gives us clothing.
- God gives us good gifts.
- We should give to God.
- We should talk with God.
- We can't see God, but he sees us.
- God listens when we pray.

BIBLE THOUGHTS FOR BABIES

God and Me	Jesus and Me	Me and My Bible	Me and My Family	Me and My Church
God is a person.	Jesus is a person.	The Bible is a special book.	I have a family.	Church is a happy place.
God loves me.	Jesus was a baby.	The Bible tells me about God and Jesus.	My family loves me.	People at church love me.
God made me.	Jesus had a family.		My family takes care of me.	I learn about God and Jesus at church.
God made everything.	Jesus loves me.			

- We should please Jesus.
- We should tell friends about Jesus.
- Jesus can do anything.

Older toddlers will also enjoy simple Bible stories. When selecting Bible stories for toddlers, tell them in words that young children can understand. It's best to use a baby or toddler Bible such as *The Toddlers Bible* (Victor Books, 1992) or *The First Step Bible* (Gold 'n' Honey Books, 1994). In her book *Guiding Your Child Toward God*, C. Sybil Waldrop offers these questions for evaluating Bible stories you're considering using with toddlers:

- What do you want children to learn from this story?
- Does this story relate to something meaningful that children are experiencing?
- Will the Bible story keep children's attention?
- Are the words understandable to children?
- Is the spiritual truth in the story clear?

Reinforce Bible stories by talking about Bible characters in regular conversation. For example, you might say, "Christopher is playing with a sheep puppet. He's taking good care of the sheep. Our Bible friend, David, took good care of his sheep, too." Look for ways to incorporate Bible stories and thoughts into playtime, snack time, and other regular nursery activities.

Bible Basics: Teaching Ideas for Babies and Toddlers

According to Sheila Halasz, effective Bible lessons for babies and toddlers should include auditory and tactile stimulation, lots of repetition of Bible stories or thoughts, and a consistent schedule. Look for a published nursery curriculum that incorporates these elements, or design your own using the following types of activities.

Bible conversation—It's natural for workers to want to talk to babies as they hold and care for them. And although infants don't understand everything that's said to them, they do associate the pleasant sound of a gentle voice with feelings of love and contentment. So instead of only babbles and coos or exclamations about baby's cuteness, encourage workers to expand their "baby talk" repertoire to include statements such as "Megan is a pretty baby. God made Megan so special" or "Cootchy-coo. I will tickle the chin God made."

For older babies and toddlers, nearly every activity can be connected to a Bible thought. For block play: "You're building with blocks. God gave you hands to pick them up and stack them." For rattles or rhythm instruments: "Shake, shake, shake. What a nice sound you're making. God gave you ears to hear that sound." For mirror play: "Who do you see? I see someone Jesus loves." The possibilities are endless!

Older babies and toddlers can also begin to interact with the Bible. Babies as young as four to six months can touch and pat a classroom Bible. When babies are able to grasp and pick up toys, let them handle a lightweight, pocket-sized Bible. As they hold the Bible, tell them that the Bible is God's special book. Walking toddlers will enjoy carrying their own Bibles around the room. Invite them to bring you their Bibles, and then help them open the Bibles and "read" a Bible thought. (You may want to mark appropriate Bible thoughts with a marker before class.) To draw even more attention to your Bible times, use the following finger play from Children's Ministry Magazine with toddlers.

Open the Bible *(clasp hands together like a closed book and then open the book by laying hands open),*
And read today. *(Make finger circles and hold up to eyes like glasses.)*
Open the Bible *(same as above),*
And learn God's way. *(Point to heaven.)*
Open the Bible *(same as above)*
And then we pray *(clasp hands to pray),*
"Thank you, God, for the Bible."

Music—Anyone can sing to a child. You don't have to have perfect pitch or even be able to carry a tune. Music is an effective teaching tool for any nursery worker. It soothes crying infants, lulls tired babies to sleep, and delights active toddlers.

What kind of music is best? That depends on the baby's age. For newborn nurseries, stick to quiet, soothing lullabies. If workers don't know any, encourage them to sing soft, familiar hymns such as "Amazing Grace" or "Jesus Loves Me." Or try one of these two Christian lullabies submitted to Children's Ministry Magazine by Lois Putnam and Connie Holman, respectively. Sing to the tune of "Rock-a-Bye Baby":

ROCK-A-BYE JESUS
Rock-a-bye Jesus,
In your wee bed.
Rock-a-bye Jesus,
Lay down your head.
Stars over you
Are shining so bright.
So rock-a-bye Jesus,
Good night, sleep tight!

GOD LOVES YOU SO
Rock-a-bye (baby's name),
God loves you so.
Rock-a-bye (baby's name),
'Cause you now know
God will be with you
Ev-er-y-where.
So go to sleep, (baby's name).
You're in God's care.

Most Christian bookstores (and even some secular book and music outlets) carry a good selection of lullaby recordings. Our favorite is the CD *Come to the Cradle* by Michael Card. Even after listening to it every night during Micah's first year, it still ministers to me each time I hear it. For a list of other recommended lullaby recordings, see page 142.

Older babies will enjoy a variety of music, including lively songs with motions you can help them do. Toddlers will love doing motions themselves or just marching around the room as you sing. Try this fun, active Bible song from Children's Ministry Magazine.

WE'RE WALKING IN GOD'S GARDEN
(to the tune of "The Bear Went
Over the Mountain")
We're walking in God's garden.
We're walking in God's garden.
We're walking in God's garden
To see what we can see.

We see a little bunny.
We see a little bunny.
We see a little bunny,
And all God made is good.
(Repeat to name additional animals.)

We see our friend, little (child's name).
We see our friend, little (child's name).
We see our friend, little (child's name),
And God made him (her) so good!

Tactile objects—Also known as manipulatives, these are any child-safe objects baby can touch, feel, and taste. Use different textured fabric squares to teach babies that God made soft things (silk, velvet, velour), shiny things (metallic fabrics), and rough things (burlap). Let babies handle animal rattles, squeakers, or stuffed animals as you tell them that God made the animals. Water, large craft feathers, and nonpoisonous plants are other baby-friendly examples of God's wondrous creations.

Books and pictures—For the youngest babies, cut apart simple board books to make individual pictures. Or mount actual photographs on poster board, and then cover them with clear, self-adhesive paper. Favorite pictures include balls, rattles, brightly colored flowers, baby faces, or simple animal pictures. Have the pictures handy as you rock babies, change them, or play with them on the floor. Tell babies that God made all the things they see in the pretty pictures.

Most bookstores carry a good variety of age-appropriate books for babies and toddlers. For durability, sturdy board books, fabric books, or washable vinyl books are best. Choose books with big, bright, realistic-looking photographs or illustrations. Babies often enjoy looking at books about familiar routines such as bedtime, bathtime, or playtime. They also love books with pictures of other babies. Books for babies should have only a few words on each page.

Books for toddlers may have up to several sentences on a page. Toddlers enjoy books that tell simple stories. They also love the surprise of lift-the-flap books, most of which can now be obtained in cardboard versions.

Since many books written for babies and toddlers are about animals, colors, numbers, shapes, babies, or family or community life, you can easily adapt them to reinforce Bible-teaching themes. Books about Noah's ark—a popular nursery theme as well as a much-loved Bible story—are widely available, even in secular bookstores. But finding other quality Christian books that are truly age-appropriate for babies and toddlers has proved to be harder than I expected. Unless you're near a large Christian book store, you may find a wider selection by contacting publishers directly.

Prayer—It's never too soon to start praying with children, but keep in mind that babies won't be able to speak their own prayers until they start to talk—usually somewhere around their first birthday. We started mealtime prayers with Micah as soon as he started solid foods, but he's just recently started to initiate prayers himself.

When you pray with babies and toddlers, use simple words that they can understand. Refer to God as "God" rather than "Lord" or "Father." Using other names will confuse babies who are only just beginning to understand that God is a person. Micah's mealtime prayer usually goes something like this: I say, "Dear God, thank you for our strawberries." After I pray, Micah says "amen" and then talks to himself for a while about God, thank you, and strawberries as I'm cleaning up the kitchen.

As children begin to join in your prayer times, don't ever force them to pray. Some children may pray enthusiastically as they thank God for Mommy, Daddy, teacher, pet, and anything else they can think of. Other children may not want to pray at all. Let children know that both responses are acceptable.

Bible conversation, music, tactile objects, books, pictures, and prayer are the building blocks of a child's young faith. When your church nursery cements these activities together with attentive care delivered by loving nursery workers, you can feel confident that you've helped families lay a foundation for their children's developing faith.

Let the Children Come

Lest anyone remain unconvinced of the importance of teaching babies and toddlers, let me tell you about a little girl named Sarah. Sarah's parents began bringing her to the church nursery at Foothills Baptist Church in Lyons, Colorado, when she was six months old. All that spring and summer, Sarah played happily with her teachers and the other children. As a toddler, she enthusiastically sang Bible songs, sometimes filling in important words, other times just sort of humming along. Her favorite song was "Sarah has a good friend. Jesus is his name."

As all babies do, Sarah grew, turned one, and eventually learned to walk. Not too long after she starting walking, she took a tumble. Then she didn't walk for a long time. Her parents and teachers weren't worried—they figured she'd just been scared by the fall and would start walking again when she was ready.

In December, when Sarah was sixteen months old, doctors discovered the real reason Sarah had stopped walking. Sarah was diagnosed with an inoperable brain tumor. She turned two that August, and died in November.

No parent, teacher, or church can ever know how long these precious little ones will be entrusted to their care. Even as I write this book, a close friend is grieving the loss of a child. In some cases, withholding teaching until two may be too late. Eternity is too precious to waste. So for heaven's sake, let the little children come. "Take them by the hand and lead them in the way of the Master."*

---

*(Ephesians 6:4b, *The Message: The New Testament in Contemporary English*, Eugene H. Peterson)

Section 5:

"OUT-GROWING" YOUR NURSERY

Developing related ministries for your parents, church, and community

GROWING IN

Knowing and serving the parents in your church

"My husband and I have chosen to keep our children (ages 18 months and 3) with us during worship services...I feel it is important for our children to learn to sit quietly and to learn how to worship as a family....We bring along quiet toys and simple snacks like Cheerios to keep them occupied...Over the course of time, they have both improved dramatically and usually make it through most of the service.

DANIELLE JONES
CHESTER, VIRGINIA

What? Babies in big church? Although it may not suit everyone, for some parents and churches, it works. Parents can participate in worship without worrying about the care their children are receiving. And church members enjoy having the little ones around. At Danielle Jones' church, the Chester Church of God, "no one minds them being in the church service at all." At Colony Friends Church in Newport News, Virginia, many of the babies "sing" along with the choir. A parent from Colony Friends said, "I've never heard anyone complain about the arrangement, and I like that the children are learning from the very beginning what church is for."

Even if your church nursery is stellar, most parents will want to bring their infants into church with them at least occasionally. Amidst the chaos that descends following the birth of a child, parents often find themselves longing to return to their earlier routines and experience some adult company. Many feel ready to return to church weeks before they'd consider leaving their infant with even a relative, much less an unfamiliar nursery attendant. So they bring baby with them. And they'll feel much better about their decision to return to church if baby is welcomed wherever they take him or her—even in the sanctuary.

Infants in church are one thing, but what about older babies and toddlers? If you've invested a lot of time preparing, equipping, and planning your nursery program, you'll want to encourage parents to leave their older babies. Babies will usually have more fun (and more learning) in an environment geared just for them. But don't just leave the babies in the nursery and forget about them. Having babies in "big church" now and then can remind church members that babies are a vital (and sometimes vocal) part of your church family. Here are some ways you can minister to parents by including babies in church.

Mothers rooms—Since babies' feeding schedules don't always coincide with service times, nursing mothers often find themselves missing out on church services. To help mothers participate in worship, many churches have set up mothers rooms. Gordon Reeder, a nursery parent who has attended several different churches in his denomination, described one of the mothers rooms he's encountered: "Usually this is a room in the back of the sanctuary with a large glass common wall. Curtains can be pulled to provide privacy and the lights are on dimmers and the service is piped in. The sound system has a local volume control so that the sound level can be turned down if necessary. Rocking chairs, cribs and toys are usually (but not always) provided." Mothers rooms can also be used for mothers to care for fussy babies who've had a hard time in the nursery that day.

If you can't provide a mothers room, consider screening off an area in your nursery for nursing mothers. Set up one or two rocking chairs, and then create a privacy screen with a room divider, folding wall, or even a collapsible folding screen. You'll be amazed how often the "nursing zone" gets used!

Baby dedications—Have parents of new babies bring their children into worship for a special dedication service. Most baby dedications include readings and questions that charge the parents and congregation to work together to raise the children to know the Lord. Baby dedications usually include prayers for the parents and children. If you want to make your baby dedication time extra-special, consider giving parents a small gift such as a Christian parenting book or a Bible. *Lord Bless My Child* by William and Nancie Carmichael

(Tyndale House Publishers, Inc., 1995) is a beautiful keepsake prayer journal with readings from a variety of inspirational writers that parents will come back to again and again.

New life Sunday—As your church sings a favorite worship song, have nursery workers bring all the babies into the worship area. Then have your pastor pray for all the babies, parents, and nursery workers. Parents will love seeing other church members smile at the sight of their beautiful children.

Church on the move—When parents have to stay home with a sick child, visit the family and deliver a sermon tape and bulletin. If the family includes a toddler, you may also want to include an age-appropriate Bible-learning project for the parents and child to do together. Parents will be glad to know they've been missed.

Parents are people too—Besides being parents, moms and dads are also regular adults in need of fellowship and encouragement. The following ministry ideas will help you encourage the parents in your church. Some of the ideas listed here are practical, some are spiritual, and some are just for fun!

Rubber duckie express—If you have a small church, you may be able to sponsor individual baby showers for expectant moms. If you have a large church (or a constant stream of babies, as our church seems to), try holding showers annually or quarterly. Twice a year at Overlake Christian Church, expectant moms are treated to "Tea for Two." The moms get to meet the nursery workers, tour the church nursery, and hear words of wisdom from experienced moms. Each mom also receives a small baby gift. Don't forget to include visitors in your shower plans—baby showers are a great way for newcomers to meet and connect with other families in your church.

Baby mugs—Take photographs of the babies in your nursery. Often. Use them in one or more of the following ways:

- Set up a "Cradle Roll" bulletin board with pictures of all the babies.

- Cut out baby pictures to create buttons for moms and dads. Put slogans on the buttons such as "I'm special. I'm a dad (mom)."

- Take pictures of babies with their parents to help nursery workers get to know whole families.

- Set up a special birth-announcement bulletin board for new babies. Put up a birth announcement along with pictures of the baby, his or her parents, and other family members.

● Set up a simple backdrop in the nursery, and take baby or family pictures. Develop the pictures, and give them to the families at little or no cost.

Parent connection—Include parents in their children's nursery experience by sending out a brief monthly newsletter. Incorporate regular columns such as

● "Amusing Baby Antics" (descriptions of nursery activities);

● "Baby Babble" (cute baby expressions or first words);

● "Happy Birthday" (birth announcements and birthdays);

● "Coming Attractions" (news about church and nursery events);

● "Who's On First Service?" (nursery volunteer staffing schedule); and

● "News You Can Use" (parenting, baby development, or other important information).

Write the newsletter yourself, or ask a worker or parent to help you. Parents make great nursery news reporters!

Dial-a-sitter—Wouldn't it be nice if when parents left the hospital with a new baby, they received a card with a name and phone number that announced, "Congratulations on the birth of your child! Your baby sitter will be..." You will make parents—especially new parents'—lives much easier if someone in your church maintains a list of baby sitters. Include any licensed day-care providers who attend your church, teenagers with nursery or baby-sitting experience, and parents who are willing to exchange child care.

Parent potpourri—Large organizations such as Mothers of Preschoolers (MOPS) or Community Bible Study (CBS) provide a variety of programming materials for parents interested in Bible study, fellowship, or support groups. CBS focuses more on Bible study and teaching; MOPS follows a "teaching format of topical interest...given from the Biblical perspective." Both groups provide age-appropriate teaching materials for toddlers and preschoolers. To start a MOPS group, contact MOPS International, Inc., at (303) 733-5353. To start a CBS group, contact the CBS National Service Center at 1-800-826-4181.

GROWING OUT

Extending your nursery ministry
into your community

*"One father cried when told Our House
would help with formula, diapers and
clothing. He said, 'I didn't know that we had
people this good in the world.' "*

Our House worker
Decatur, Georgia

As I was visiting Columbia Presbyterian Church in Georgia, I noticed a nice playground nearby. Micah noticed it, too, and headed straight for it. When I asked Columbia pastor Joan Gray to tell me about the facility, she simply said, "Oh. That's Our House." Our House?

Joan went on to explain that Our House is a day-care center for homeless children. Columbia Presbyterian "leases" a small building on its campus to Our House—for one dollar per year. Our House was started when a group of homeless-shelter volunteers from another church in town grew increasingly concerned about the needs of homeless families with children. They formed a task force, mobilized others in their community, and eventually Our House became a reality. Since 1988, Our House has provided state-licensed care for up to eight infants, ten toddlers, and twenty preschoolers—at no cost to their parents. What an important ministry!

The children in your church need to know about Jesus' love. But what about the babies and parents outside your church walls? Communities everywhere are filled with families who have never experienced God's love. For whatever reason, they don't feel a need to hear sermons or sing hymns, but they do need diapers and clothing for their babies. They need loving child care so they can go to work. They need help to become the loving parents they want to be. And Jesus calls Christians in churches to meet these needs.

Our House is a great organization, but it took a lot of people and a lot of time to get it up and running. When I spoke with Our House director Paige McKay, she suggested a host of more immediate ways churches could make a difference in these families' lives.

Have a diaper drive. Encourage church members to bring disposable diapers and donate them to a local family shelter or low-income child-care facility. You could also collect formula and baby food.

Sponsor a homeless child in your church's child-care program. Collect financial contributions to cover a year's tuition. If your church doesn't have its own day-care facilities, make arrangements with another church or community facility.

Encourage church members to volunteer. Our House uses volunteers as teachers aids, or to help new children adjust to the Our House program. Homeless shelters and community day-care centers in your community probably have similar needs. Volunteers planning to work with children should be prepared to fill out applications and provide references for background checking.

Hold a churchwide workday. Offer to help local family service agencies with painting, landscaping, or general maintenance projects.

Invite a day care to lunch. Sponsor a summer family picnic in a local park. Have church members provide the food. Invite the families of children from a low-income day-care center to join you.

Need more ideas? The following ministries will benefit parents in your church, as well as others in your community.

Diapers to diplomas—After Micah was born, Tom and I gathered all the baby-care information we'd received from the doctor and hospital and put it in a folder. We called the folder "Micah's Instruction Manual." It was somewhat helpful but was by no means an exhaustive guide to all the situations we'll encounter.

Parenting is one of life's greatest joys but also one of its greatest challenges. In response to this challenge, hospitals, community organizations, and churches offer parenting classes. And parents are coming in droves. People who would otherwise never set foot in a church may be willing to come for a parenting class.

When you set up your parenting classes, remember that there are different stages of parenting. Although some parenting skills may apply to children of all ages, participants will glean more from classes that focus on specific parenting topics. Parents of babies, toddlers, school-aged children, and teenagers will benefit from separate classes that are small enough to allow for participant discussion.

Moms (or dads!) day out—At First United Methodist Church in Clinton, Oklahoma, every Wednesday is Mothers Day Out. So is Thursday. For ten dollars, parents from the church and community can leave their children at the church from 9 a.m. to 3 p.m. The parents provide a lunch, and the church provides age-appropriate crafts, games, and songs for the children. Fees are used to pay child-care providers and purchase supplies as needed.

When Nancy Rodolph, children's ministries director at First United Methodist, told me about this program, all I could say was "wow." As a mom who works part time at home, I've often wished for a safe and caring place where I could leave Micah while I run errands, clean the house (or church nursery), or finish up a project. I had just about convinced myself that no such thing existed when Nancy Rodolph told me about her program. Since then, I've called around and found a couple of churches in our community that offer a similar service. They'll be seeing us soon!

The baby exchange—Parents from all walks of life will benefit from an organized baby-clothing share program because of this indisputable fact of life: Babies completely outgrow and/or destroy everything in their closet within three or four months. At this point, most parents either store the clothes for future use by another child (their own or a friend or family member's), give them away, or have a garage sale. Baby clothes aren't getting any cheaper. Why not get the church involved and help parents share the wealth of baby clothing and other supplies they've accumulated?

To begin, decide what types of items you'll accept (clothing or other items; new or used; excellent, good, or fair condition). Then choose a place to store the items. If you don't have room in your church, ask a volunteer to keep the items at home. Let people in your church and community know what items are available and who might benefit most from them.

Teen mom ministry—Teenage mothers need a lot of help. They barely know how to take care of themselves, much less a helpless baby. A teenage mother's decision to keep her baby may cause family, friends, or classmates to reject her. Finishing school and finding suitable employment (and child care) can be tough. Even coming to church can be a frightening experience—and another possible source of rejection.

The problem looms large—so large it may seem impossible to make a difference. But around the country, Christian organizations such as Youth for Christ and Caring Pregnancy Center are teaming up with community volunteers to help teen moms learn parenting and other life skills. Such programs provide baby showers where girls and their babies feel loved and accepted, support groups where girls can meet and share experiences with other teen moms, and older mentor moms to befriend and encourage teens on their parenting journey. For information about joining or starting a program in your area, contact: Jill Meyer, Teen Mom Director, Denver Area Youth For Christ, Inc., P.O. Box 101600, Denver, CO 80250.

My heart warms to think of these and the myriad other ways churches can minister to young children and their families. Jesus didn't just accept children, he actively loved them. He took them in his arms, touched them, and blessed them. When I read these accounts, I imagine children running excitedly back to their parents with shouts of "Mommy! Daddy! Jesus touched me!"

Although Jesus isn't here to physically touch the children in our churches and communities, he still touches children through our work. We are the body of Christ. And when we reach beyond the walls of our churches to offer encouragement and service to sometimes struggling families, we are Jesus' hands in our communities.

Through our ministries, his hands can

...hold precious gifts from God,

...touch tiny hearts with his love,

...help hurting families, and

...lovingly embrace even the most unlovable child.

Little children are truly gifts from God. I pray that this book has helped you as you minister to the babies and families in your church. May God bless each child, parent, worker, congregation, and community that comes into contact with your safe and caring nursery as you joyfully serve in Jesus' name.

Appendix 1

....

FIRST AID, EMERGENCY, AND SICKNESS POLICIES

"I stopped going because my church does not do anything about parents who bring their sick kids to the baby-sitting."

JANET

EUCLID, OHIO

I sympathize with Janet. Any time we're about to leave for a trip, I keep Micah out of the nursery, just in case. And when Micah does come down with something, I always wonder whether he could have picked it up at church. He doesn't go to day care, and he's too young for play dates. Where else could all these nasty little viruses be hiding?

Anywhere, really. Behind his ears, under his bed. Little children seem to have a mysterious talent for breeding germs. Especially during the winter cold and flu season, parents may feel like their child will never be well—at least not on a Sunday. Then, after several weeks of missing church to stay home with a sick child, something snaps and they resolve to get the whole family to church, germs or no germs.

Sound the Germ Alert!

No nursery is ever 100 percent germ-free. Parents may unknowingly bring sick children before they exhibit any symptoms. Workers assigned to clean toys may occasionally miss one or two that have been mouthed. From time to time, these things happen and there's not much you can do to prevent them. But you can prevent one obvious source of germs: visibly sick children.

Although it may seem harsh, sick children should not be allowed in your nursery. When parents show up with a child who appears to be sick, workers should kindly explain their concern for the health of all the children in your program and invite the parents to bring the child back when he or she is well. If a child becomes sick while in the nursery, a worker should contact his or her parents immediately. As you wait for parents to arrive, try to keep the child away from other children.

How sick is too sick? In general, you should refuse sick children with the following symptoms:

- fever within the previous twenty-four hours;
- vomiting and/or diarrhea within the previous twenty-four hours;
- any symptoms of childhood diseases such as scarlet fever, measles, mumps, chicken pox, or whooping cough;
- runny nose with any colored discharge;
- sore throat;
- any unexplained rash;
- any skin infection;
- pink eye and other eye infections; or
- head lice (child should be free of all nits).

Once you've developed a sick-child policy for your nursery, post it where parents will see it. (Create your own or use the sample "Sorry You're Sick" policy on page 135.) Then start enforcing it. No one wants the church nursery to turn into a germ factory. Except for the most extenuating circumstances ("I had to bring him because my husband is out of town and I couldn't find anyone to teach my Sunday school class"), parents aren't likely to question workers' enforcement of an established sick-child policy. And if they do, simply remind them of the Golden Rule: Do unto other parents as you would have them do unto you.

Bring on the Band-Aids

Unlike most childhood illnesses, injuries aren't contagious. But you do need to be prepared to deal with them as they arise. Keep a stocked first-aid kit in each nursery or toddler room. Be sure to keep first-aid kits out of children's reach. In addition to adhesive bandages and antibiotic ointment, you may want to include the following supplies:

- adhesive tape,
- alcohol swabs,

- antiseptic solution,
- cotton balls,
- cotton swabs (Q-Tips),
- gauze pads,
- hydrogen peroxide,
- hydrocortisone cream,
- instant ice packs,
- ipecac syrup,
- scissors (for cutting gauze or tape),
- steri-slips (butterfly adhesive bandages),
- a sewing needle (for removing splinters), and
- tweezers.

NURSERY NOTE

Infant and child CPR training is beyond the scope of this book. It must be delivered by a trained, certified instructor and is readily available in most areas through hospitals, the American Heart Association, or the American Red Cross. To best ensure children's safety in your nursery, always have at least one trained infant and child CPR provider in your church building or nursery area when children are present. Better yet, arrange for all nursery workers to attend CPR training once a year.

Hugs and Band-Aids will remedy most minor nursery hurts. Bumps, bruises, and scrapes are commonplace events in the life of a child. Some babies who take a tumble while playing may not even notice. But if a child really gets hurt, he or she should be treated with appropriate first aid. You can post the "First-Aid Fact Sheets" (pp. 136-138) in your nursery to provide workers with appropriate treatments for common injuries they might encounter. Call your local chapter of the American Red Cross for more information about first aid. (If you don't have a local chapter, call the American National Red Cross at (703) 206-6000 or visit the Red Cross Web site at http://www.crossnet.org.) Even better, ask them about first-aid classes that are available in your community.

Beyond Band-Aids

Any time a child is seriously hurt, parents should be notified as soon as possible. Have one worker stay with the injured child while a fellow teacher notifies the child's parents and appropriate church staff (such as a nursery coordinator, children's pastor, or pastor). If the injury is serious enough to require immediate medical attention, church staff may choose to call for emergency services, (or a doctor in your church, if available) before notifying parents.

After the appropriate people have been notified, have workers...

- remain calm.
- reassure all the children, including the injured child.
- remove other children from the area as soon as possible.
- make a detailed written report of the accident, including all available information about what happened.

Accidents are serious business. Your nursery manual needs to include detailed procedures for handling accidents and injuries. As you develop your accident policies, be sure to consult appropriate legal and medical personnel, or use a resource such as The Good Shepherd Program. Your parents—and your workers—will thank you.

••

Sorry You're Sick

In order to provide a safe, healthy nursery for all our nursery children, we ask that you keep your baby or toddler at home any time he or she exhibits the following symptoms:

❑ fever within the previous twenty-four hours;

❑ vomiting and/or diarrhea within the previous twenty-four hours;

❑ any symptoms of childhood diseases such as scarlet fever, measles, mumps, chicken pox, or whooping cough;

❑ runny nose with any colored discharge;

❑ sore throat;

❑ any unexplained rash;

❑ any skin infection;

❑ pink eye and other eye infections; or

❑ head lice (child should be free of all nits).

Thank you for your cooperation. We hope your child feels better soon!

••

FIRST-AID FACT SHEET

Contact parents before treating any of these injuries.

Bumps and Bruises
- Elevate bruised arms or legs.
- Apply an ice pack or cold compress to the bumped or bruised area.
- Continue as long as baby will permit, taking a break every fifteen minutes, up to an hour.
- For bumps on the head, call for emergency medical assistance if the child exhibits any of these symptoms:
    - loss of consciousness;
    - convulsions;
    - vomiting;
    - black-and-blue areas around the eyes or behind the ears;
    - difficulty breathing, moving, or seeing; or
    - blood or fluid flowing from the ears or nose.

Burns
- Treat minor burns by immersing the burned area in cool water. Apply cold compresses to burns on the trunk or face areas.
- Don't apply ice, butter, or medication.
- After soaking, gently pat the area dry and cover with a nonstick bandage.
- For serious burns, get immediate emergency medical attention.

Cuts
For scrapes:
- Gently sponge off the wound with soap and water.
- Apply direct pressure with a clean cloth if the bleeding doesn't stop on its own.
- Cover with a sterile bandage.

For minor cuts:
- Clean with soap and water.
- Hold the cut under running water to flush out any remaining dirt.
- Cover with a sterile bandage. To keep the cut closed, use a butterfly bandage.

For major cuts:
- Call for emergency medical assistance.
- Apply direct pressure with a clean cloth, gauze pad, or your finger if necessary. Elevate the wound above the heart, if possible.

Electric Shock

- Do not touch the child or the electrical item causing the shock.
- If possible, break contact with the current by turning off the electricity.
- If power cannot be turned off, gently separate the child from the current by using a dry, nonmetallic object such as a broom, chair, cushion, or large book.
- Do not touch the child until he or she is away from the current.
- Call for emergency medical assistance.

Insect Bites

- Scrape off honeybee stingers with your fingernail or the blunt edge of a knife. Don't try to grab the stinger; this could force more venom into baby's skin.
- Wash minor bee, wasp, ant, or spider bites with soap and water. Then apply cold compresses.
- Apply calamine lotion to mosquito bites or other itchy bites.
- If a baby breaks out in hives or experiences breathing difficulty, hoarseness, coughing, wheezing, severe headache, nausea, vomiting, thickened tongue, facial swelling, weakness, dizziness, or fainting following a bee sting or insect bite, get immediate emergency medical attention. These symptoms could indicate an allergic reaction.

Nosebleeds

- Try to calm baby.
- Hold baby upright or leaning slightly forward.
- Gently pinch both nostrils between your thumb and index finger for five to ten minutes.

Pinched Fingers or Toes

- Elevate and apply ice to the pinched finger or toe.
- Check bruised extremities for discoloration, bleeding under the nail, deep cuts, or misshapen fingers or toes. Advise parents to consult their physician if any of these conditions are present.
- Immobilize suspected fractured or dislocated extremities with a makeshift splint until a doctor can be seen.
- Don't try to move fractured or dislocated extremities back into alignment.

Poison

- Call your local poison-control center immediately. Carefully follow all instructions you receive.
- Do not induce vomiting unless the poison-control center instructs you to do so.

Splinters

- Wash the area with soap and water.
- Numb the area with an ice pack or cold compress.
- Sterilize a sewing needle and tweezers with alcohol swabs.
- If the splinter is completely embedded, use a sterilized sewing needle to gently work it loose.
- If one end of the splinter is clearly visible, try to remove it with sterilized tweezers.
- Wash the area again after you have removed the splinter.

Appendix 2

HOW TO CARE FOR CHILDREN WITH SPECIAL NEEDS

"The government mandate now is for full inclusion. Can't the church do as well or better?"

BARBARA CURTIS
NOVATO, CALIFORNIA

Barbara Curtis is a professional author, speaker, educator. She's also the mother of eleven children. Oh, yes. And three of her children have Down syndrome. As we talked about her church nursery experiences, she suggested that church nursery programs serving special-needs children keep the communication lines open—with parents, with workers, and with the Lord.

Communicate openly with parents. "It's very disconcerting for parents to experience weird vibes," Barbara said. Parents of special-needs children would much rather be asked straightforward questions about their children's needs. Helpful questions include:

- What special needs does your child have?
- What activities does your child most enjoy?
- What activities would you like your child to avoid, if any?
- Does your child require any special equipment?
- Which nursery classroom would meet your child's needs best?

Communicate openly with workers. Many people seem to have a fear of special-needs children. A little training can go a long way in dispelling these fears. If you have special-needs children in your nursery, you can start by educating yourself about their disabilities. Go to the library and read up on Down syndrome, cerebral palsy, and other disabilities you might encounter. Invite parents of special-needs children to address workers at training meetings.

Communicate openly with the Lord. Pray that God will remove your fears and allow you to shower special-needs children with his love. Ask the Holy Spirit to show you what actions will best minister to these special children and their families—and to give you the courage to do them. Listen to the words of Scripture:

"Sons are a heritage from the Lord, children a reward from him" (Psalm 127:3).

"For you created my inmost being; you knit me together in my mother's womb. I praise you because I am fearfully and wonderfully made; your works are wonderful, I know that full well" (Psalm 139:13-14).

"I tell you the truth, whatever you did for one of the least of these brothers of mine, you did for me" (Matthew 25:40b).

"Those parts of the body that seem to be weaker are indispensable, and the parts that we think are less honorable we treat with special honor" (1 Corinthians 12:22b-23a).

Once you've got the communication lines flowing, try these specific ideas as you work with the special-needs children in your nursery.

● Unless parents direct you to do otherwise, place special-needs children in the same class as their peers.

● Special-needs children may require individualized attention. Plan for extra workers, if possible.

● Allow special-needs children to complete activities themselves whenever possible.

● Use lots of repetition (a sound teaching technique for all young children!).

● Plan activities that use multiple senses so that children with a disability in one area (loss of vision, hearing, motion) won't be excluded.

● Adapt your room and equipment as needed. The Sources for Nursery Materials appendix (pp. 141-142) includes sources for special-needs adaptable equipment.

May you receive special blessings as you minister to these special children!

Appendix 3

SOURCES FOR NURSERY MATERIALS

Child Development

Eisenberg, Arlene, et al. *What to Expect the First Year*. New York, NY: Workman Publishing Company, Inc., 1994.

Eisenberg, Arlene, et al. *What to Expect the Toddler Years*. New York, NY: Workman Publishing Company, Inc., 1994.

Lansdown, Richard, et al. *Your Child's Development From Birth Through Adolescence*. New York, NY: Alfred A. Knopf, 1991.

Miller, Karen. *Ages and Stages: Developmental Descriptions & Activities, Birth Through Eight Years*. Chelsea, MA: Telshare Publishing, Inc., 1985.

Curriculum and Teaching

Beers, V. Gilbert. *Teaching Toddlers the Bible*. Wheaton, IL: Victor Books, 1993.

Curtis, Barbara. *Small Beginnings*. Nashville, TN: Broadman & Holman Publishers, 1997.

Haystead, Wes. *Teaching Your Child About God*. Ventura, CA: Regal Books, 1995.

Mahand, Melinda, et al. *Love, Laughter, and Learning*. Nashville, TN: Convention Press, 1996.

Roehlkepartain, Jolene L. *Children's Ministry That Works!* Loveland, CO: Group Publishing, Inc., 1991.

Seaton, Kathleen Lull, et al. *Early Childhood Ministry and Your Church*. Minneapolis, MN: Augsberg Fortress, 1991.

Waldrop, C. Sybil. *Guiding Your Child Toward God*. Nashville, TN: Broadman & Holman Publishers, 1984.

Paschang, Debbie, et al. *The Nurturing Nursery*. Elgin, IL: David C. Cook Publishing Co., 1992.

Games and Activities

Lansky, Vicki. *Games Babies Play From Birth to Twelve Months*. Deephaven, MN: The Book Peddlers, 1993.

Lingo, Susan L. *Age-Right Play*. Loveland, CO: Group Publishing, Inc., 1997.

Miller, Karen. *More Things to Do With Toddlers and Twos*. Chelsea, MA: Telshare Publishing, Inc., 1990.

Reitzes, Fretta, et al. *Wonderplay: Interactive & Developmental Games, Crafts, & Creative Activities for Infants, Toddlers, & Preschoolers*. Philadelphia, PA: Running Press, 1995.

Silberg, Jackie. *Games to Play With Babies*. Mount Rainier, MD: Gryphon House, Inc., 1993.

Silberg, Jackie. *Games to Play With Toddlers*. Mount Rainier, MD: Gryphon House, Inc., 1993.

Toys and Equipment

The following mail-order companies offer toys for babies and toddlers. Companies marked with an asterisk (*) also offer other nursery equipment.

Back to Basics Toys
31333 Agoura Road
Westlake Village, CA 91361-4639
1-800-356-5360

Constructive Playthings
1227 East 119th Street
Grandview, MO 64030-1117
1-800-832-0572

Discovery Toys, Inc.
Martinez, CA 94553
1-800-426-4777

Hand in Hand
891 Main Street
Oxford, ME 04270-9711
1-800-872-9745

The Natural Baby Company*
816 Silvia Street, 800 B-S
Trenton, NJ 08628-3299
(609) 771-9233

One Step Ahead*
P.O. Box 517
Lake Bluff, IL 60044
1-800-274-8440

Perfectly Safe*
7835 Freedom Avenue NW, Suite 3
North Canton, OH 44720-6907
1-800-837-5437
www.4perfectlysafe.com

PlayFair Toys
P.O. Box 18210
Boulder, CO 80308
1-800-824-7255

The Right Start*
5334 Sterling Center Drive
Westlake Village, CA 91361-4627
1-800-548-8531

Sensational Beginnings
P.O. Box 2009
987 Stewart Road
Monroe, MI 48162
1-800-444-2147

Music

Angels All Around: Gentle Blessings. Nashville, TN: Word, Inc., 1996.

Angels All Around: Peaceful Prayers. Nashville, TN: Word, Inc., 1996.

Angels All Around: Soothing Scriptures. Nashville, TN: Word, Inc., 1996.

Bach at Bedtime. New York, NY: Philips Classics Production, 1995.

Card, Michael. Come to the Cradle. Brentwood, TN: The Sparrow Corporation, 1993.

Card, Michael. Sleep Sound in Jesus. Chatsworth, CA: The Sparrow Corporation, 1989.

Mozart for Babies. Klick Verlag, Switzerland: Perleberg Music International, 1995.

Bibles and Other Devotional Books for Babies*

Baby's First Bible. Cincinnati, OH: The Standard Publishing Company, 1996.

Beers, V. Gilbert. The Toddlers Bible. Wheaton, IL: Victor Books, 1992.

Butterworth, Nick, et al. I Wonder... book series. Wheaton, IL: Victor Books.

Field, Rachel. Prayer for a Child. New York, NY: Little Simon, 1997.

The First Step Bible. Sisters, OR: Questar Publishers, Inc., 1994.

Harrast, Tracy L. My Mommy and Me Story Bible. Grand Rapids, MI: Zondervan Publishing House, 1995.

Hollingsworth, Mary. The Story of Jesus. Sisters, OR: Questar Publishers, Inc., 1995.

Hollingsworth, Mary. What Does Jesus Say? Sisters, OR: Questar Publishers, Inc., 1995.

Hollingsworth, Mary. Who Is Jesus? Sisters, OR: Questar Publishers, Inc., 1995.

My First Prayers book series. Newmarket, England: Brimax Books Ltd.

Pray and Play Bible for Young Children. Loveland, CO: Group Publishing, Inc., 1997.

Simon, Mary Manz. Hear Me Read Bible Stories series. St. Louis, MO: Concordia Publishing House.

Simon, Mary Manz. Little Visits for Toddlers. St. Louis, MO: Concordia Publishing House, 1990.

Stanley, Andy and Sandra. The Toddler's ABC Book. Nashville, TN: Thomas Nelson, Inc., 1995.

*By no means an exhaustive list, but after months of looking, these are some of the best I've found. Many are available in sturdy board book editions.

Special-Needs Publications

Exceptional Parent magazine
1-800-562-1973

Oppenheim Toy Portfolio
1-800-544-TOYS
http://www.toyportfolio.com

Oppenheim, Joanne. Oppenheim Toy Portfolio: The Best Toys, Books, Videos & Software for Kids, 1997. Rocklin, CA: Prima Publishing, 1997.

Special-Needs Catalogs

Achievement for Children and Adults
    With Special Needs
    (412) 444-6400

Dragonfly Toy Company
    1-800-654-5548

Flaghouse
    1-800-221-5185

Jesana Ltd.
    1-800-443-4728

Kapable Kids
    1-800-356-1564

Lakeshore
    1-800-421-5354

Toys for Special Children
    (914) 478-0960

Group Publishing, Inc.
Attention: Books & Curriculum
P.O. Box 481, Loveland, CO 80539
Fax: (970) 669-1994

Evaluation for *THE SAFE AND CARING CHURCH NURSERY*

Please help Group Publishing, Inc., continue to provide innovative and useful resources for ministry. Please take a moment to fill out this evaluation and mail or fax it to us. Thanks!

● ● ●

1. As a whole, this book has been (circle one)

not very helpful   very helpful

1   2   3   4   5   6   7   8   9   10

2. The best things about this book:

3. Ways this book could be improved:

4. Things I will change because of this book:

5. Other books I'd like to see Group publish in the future:

6. Would you be interested in field-testing future Group products and giving us your feedback? If so, please fill in the information below:

Name _____

Street Address _____

City _____

State _____

Zip _____

Phone Number_____ Date_____

TEACH YOUR PRESCHOOLERS AS JESUS TAUGHT WITH GROUP'S *HANDS-ON BIBLE CURRICULUM*™

Hands-On Bible Curriculum™ **for preschoolers** helps your preschoolers learn the way they learn best—by touching, exploring, and discovering. With active learning, preschoolers love learning about the Bible, and they really remember what they learn.

Because small children learn best through repetition, Preschoolers and Pre-K & K will learn one important point per lesson, and Toddlers & 2s will learn one point each month with **Hands-On Bible Curriculum**. These important lessons will stick with them and comfort them during their daily lives. Your children will learn:
- •God is our friend,
- •who Jesus is, and
- •we can always trust Jesus.

The **Learning Lab®** is packed with age-appropriate learning tools for fun, faith-building lessons. Toddlers & 2s explore big **Interactive StoryBoards**™ with enticing textures that toddlers love to touch—like sandpaper for earth, cotton for clouds, and blue cellophane for water. While they hear the Bible story, children also *touch* the Bible story. And they learn. **Bible Big Books**™ captivate Preschoolers and Pre-K & K while teaching them important Bible lessons. With **Jumbo Bible Puzzles**™ and involving **Learning Mats**™, your children will see, touch, and explore their Bible stories. Each quarter there's a brand new collection of supplies to keep your lessons fresh and involving.

Fuzzy, age-appropriate hand puppets are also available to add to the learning experience. What better way to teach your class than with the help of an attention-getting teaching assistant? These child-friendly puppets help you teach each lesson with scripts provided in the **Teacher Guide**. Plus, your children will enjoy teaching the puppets what they learn. Cuddles the Lamb, Whiskers the Mouse, and Pockets the Kangaroo turn each lesson into an interactive and entertaining learning experience.

Just order one **Learning Lab** and one **Teacher Guide** for each age level, add a few common classroom supplies, and presto—you have everything you need to inspire and build faith in your children. For more interactive fun, introduce your children to the age-appropriate puppet who will be your teaching assistant and their friend. No student books are required!

Hands-On Bible Curriculum is also available for elementary grades.

Order today from your local Christian bookstore, or write:
Group Publishing, P.O. Box 485, Loveland, CO 80539.